Thank's for a
most interesting
Taxi ride.
    Best wishs
    Dave Watts

About the author
Russell Ash has lived in London for the first two and the past eighteen years of his life, with a childhood in Bedford and a university education in Durham between. He is the author of books on such diverse subjects as highwaymen, the Impressionists and the Wright Brothers. Among his recent books are *The Cynic's Dictionary*, *The Official British Yuppie Handbook* and *Last Laughs*. He is also the co-author, with Brian Lake, of *Bizarre Books*.

THE
LONDONER'S ALMANAC

Russell Ash

CENTURY PUBLISHING

LONDON

First published in Great Britain in 1985
by Century Publishing Co. Ltd,
Portland House,
12–13 Greek Street, London W1V 5LE

ISBN 0 7126 0928 8

Photoset by Rowland Phototypesetting Ltd,
Bury St Edmunds, Suffolk

Printed in Great Britain in 1985 by
Hunt Barnard Printing Co., Aylesbury, Bucks

My thanks to all the organizations and individuals who so
helpfully supplied information – especially those named in
connection with specially prepared lists.
My particular thanks to Lucy Trench, who helped me with
the research and whose efficiency saved me from drowning in
a sea of notes.

CONTENTS

INTRODUCTION

I compiled this book because there are 'Books of Lists' of just about everything you can think of: food, royalty, cinema – even a *Book of Texas Lists* – but not one of London, which seemed shabby treatment for such an important and fascinating city.

My choice of subjects is completely arbitrary. It reflects as broad as possible a range, but there simply wasn't room for everything. I would be pleased to hear of any glaring omissions – together with any new lists you might like to suggest – for inclusion in future editions of this book.

PATRICK ROBERTSON'S
TEN FAVOURITE LONDON FIRSTS

1 The first cheque

The first known cheque was drawn on Messrs Clayton & Morris, bankers of Cornhill, and made out for £10 by Nicholas Vanacker on 22 April 1659. Just a scrap of paper, but it marks the beginning of banking as we know it today. It was sold at Sotheby's for £1300 in 1976.

2 The first roller skates

Roller skates were worn for the first time by a Belgian musical instrument maker called Joseph Merlin at a masquerade held at Carlisle House, Soho Square, in 1760. Merlin came sailing into the ballroom on his roller skates playing a violin. Unable to change direction or retard his velocity, he crashed into a large mirror valued at £500, smashed it to atoms, broke his instrument and wounded himself severely.

3 The first shop with plate glass windows

This was a men's outfitters established by Francis Place, the pioneer birth-controller, at 16 Charing Cross on 8 April 1801. Accused of reckless extravagance, Place rejoined that he '. . . sold from the windows more goods . . . than paid the journeymen's wages and the expenses of housekeeping'. His innovation helped to transform the shopping streets of London from their eighteenth-century appearance to what we have today.

4 The first city to reach a population of one million

London was the world's first great metropolis. It topped a million in 1811, when the census recorded a population of 1 009 546 people. It remained the largest city in the world until 1957, when it was overtaken by Tokyo. The Big Apple was never the biggest – eat your heart out, New York . . .

5 The first public lavatory

Known euphemistically as a 'Public Waiting Room', the first gents was opened at 95 Fleet Street by the Society of Arts on

2 February 1852. Its two principal instigators were both celebrated in other fields – Sir Samuel Merton Peto was the building contractor who erected Nelson's Column and Sir Henry Cole produced the first Christmas card. The price of admission, incidentally, was twopence – 'spending a penny' had to wait until the first municipal lavatory opened outside the Royal Exchange in 1855.

6 The first traffic island

London's first traffic island was privately installed in St James's Street by Colonel Pierpoint in 1864, so that he would be able to reach the haven of his club without accident. The gallant Colonel was wont to gaze over his shoulder to admire his island as he crossed the street, which on one notable occasion caused him to be knocked over by a cab.

7 The first escalator

Installed in Harrods in 1898 because the manager had an intense dislike of lifts, the first escalator proved such a moving experience for many who rode on it that an attendant had to be stationed at the top to dispense brandy or sal volatile respectively to gentlemen or ladies overcome by terror. When the first escalator at an underground station was opened at Earls Court in 1911, the District Railway engaged 'Bumper' Harris, a man with a wooden leg, to ride up and down it all day to instil confidence in the faint-hearted.

8 The first multi-storey car park

Much earlier than most people might imagine, this was opened at 6 Denman Street, just off Piccadilly Circus, in May 1901. There were seven floors and a hydraulic lift capable of raising a three-ton lorry to the top storey. It is interesting in showing that even at this time there must have been severe parking problems in London. It is also surprising that there were enough cars around at that time to fill its 19000 square feet of floor space.

9 The first cocktail party

Alec Waugh, brother of novelist Evelyn, threw this at the Haverstock Hill studio of painter C. W. Nevinson on 26 April

1924. Unfortunately, so novel was the idea of drinks at 5.30 p.m., that only one guest turned up. The next venture was more successful – Waugh invited thirty people to tea but gave them potent cocktails instead. Everyone drank themselves silly, had a wonderful time, and started giving cocktail parties themselves.

10   The first video recordings
These went on sale at Major Radiovision of Wigmore Street in June 1935. No, that is not a misprint – home video really did exist in the mid-1930s. The video discs cost seven shillings each and were designed to be played on a videorecorder attached to a low-definition TV set. They gave six minutes of recorded sound and vision on each side.

[Patrick Robertson is the author of *The Shell Book of Firsts* (revised edition published by Michael Joseph, 1984) which lists every conceivable and many inconceivable firsts from all over the world.]

LONDON'S TEN MOST POPULAR MUSEUMS AND ART GALLERIES [1984]

	Visitors
British Museum	3 236 719
Science Museum	3 019 892
National Gallery	2 936 926
Natural History Museum	2 317 750
Jewel House, Tower of London	1 746 085
Victoria and Albert Museum	1 629 813
Tate Gallery	1 265 605
Royal Academy of Arts	904 065
Imperial War Museum	696 288
Museum of London	528 958

THE TEN COMMONEST CAUSES OF COMPLAINT IN LONDON MUSEUMS AND ART GALLERIES

1 The state of the lavatories ('disgusting').
2 The lighting in the galleries ('sepulchral').
3 The labelling of exhibits ('too high'; 'too low'; 'too obscure'; 'in French').
4 Direction signs ('confusing'; 'aren't any').
5 The restaurant or tea-room ('excessively twee'; 'outrageous price for a cup of tea').
6 Staff: *Wardens* ('elusive'; 'don't speak a word of English').
   Curators ('affected accents'; 'elitist'; 'patronizing').
7 Opening hours ('inconvenient').
8 Expense of visiting a special exhibition ('monstrous').
9 Drunks and vagrants lurking in galleries annoying bona fide visitors.
10 Favourite object not available as a postcard (unless it is a fourteenth-century Tibetan rain-bucket – see also *Bestselling Postcards in the Victoria and Albert Museum*, page 15).

[List compiled specially for *The Londoner's Almanac* by a London museum official, who prefers to remain anonymous.]

NO. 1 BESTSELLING POSTCARDS IN LONDON MUSEUMS AND ART GALLERIES

British Museum
Rosetta Stone

Imperial War Museum
HMS Belfast

Museum of London
Lord Mayor's Coach

National Gallery
Leonardo cartoon

National Portrait Gallery
Virginia Woolf
(Margaret Thatcher is now
in the top 5.)

Natural History Museum
Photograph of the Museum

Science Museum
'New Humber' lavatory, c1880

Tate Gallery
Norham Castle by Turner

BESTSELLING POSTCARDS IN THE VICTORIA AND ALBERT MUSEUM

1 Royal Doulton lavatory advertisement
2 *Salisbury Cathedral* by John Constable
3 *Venice: San Salute in the Distance* by J. M. W. Turner
4 *The Miraculous Draught of Fishes* by Raphael
5 The Ardabill Carpet
6 *Young Man Among Roses* by Nicholas Hilliard
7 The Great Bed of Ware
8 Tippoo's Tiger
9 *Cottage in a Cornfield* by John Constable
10 Exterior of the Victoria and Albert Museum (photograph)

The least bestselling postcard in the Victoria and Albert
Museum is one depicting a fourteenth-century Tibetan
rain-bucket. In 1979, in a temporary fit of euphoria,
Publications Officer Mr Nicky Bird had 5000 printed. Of
these, twenty-four were subsequently destroyed in a flood
and just four sold – an average of less than one a year.
Anyone with 4972 friends who might like to receive a
picture of this remarkable exhibit may well be able to
come to an arrangement with Mr Bird, c/o the V and A.

Sotheby's: Ten Auction Record Prices

1 Record for any London sale
The Robert von Hirsch Collection, June 1978: £18 468 348.

2 Record for any work of art
The Gospels of Henry the Lion, 6 December 1983: £8 140 000.

3 Record for a painting
JMW Turner's *Seascape: Folkestone*, 5 July 1984: £7 370 000.

4 Record for a piece of silver
'Shield of Achilles', 3 May 1984: £484 000.

5 Record for European porcelain
Sèvres 'Rose Pompadour' ewer and basin, 12 June 1984: £126 000.

6 Record for costume
Costume from Diaghilev Ballet, 9 May 1984: £28 600.

7 Record for a toy
Marklin tinplate 'Rocket' train set, made in Germany, c1909, 29 May 1984: £28 050.

8 Record for a doll
William and Mary doll of c1690, 29 May 1984: £17 600.

9 Record for golf club and ball
Eighteenth-century club, 24 July 1984: £4620; a ball of c1840: £2200.

10 Record for an item of fishing tackle
A 2.5-inch 1891 'Perfect' trout reel, 2 May 1984: £3630.

TEN PERSONAL ITEMS AUCTIONED BY SOTHEBY'S IN RECENT YEARS

1   Swedenborg's skull
A skull, said to be that of the Swedish philosopher, Emanuel Swedenborg (1688–1772) was sold on 6 March 1978 for £1500.

2   George Bernard Shaw's gardening gloves
Sold on 16 October 1978 for £28 – believed to be a record price for a pair of gardening gloves belonging to an author.

3   Charles Dickens' ivory pencil
Sold on 6 July 1977 for £110.

4   Virginia Woolf's tortoise-shell spectacles
Sold on 10 November 1980 for £250.

5   Henry II's suit of armour
Sold on 5 May 1983 for £1 925 000 – a world auction record.

6   John Lennon's 'Imagine'
On 1 September 1983 the handwritten lyrics of this 1971 song made £7150. At the same sale John Lennon's Broadwood upright piano fetched £9900.

7   Elvis Presley at Las Vegas souvenir menus
Five were auctioned on 1 September 1983 for £55.

8   Mahler's First Symphony
His manuscript was sold on 10 May 1984 for £143 000.

9   Madame de Pompadour's watering-cans
A pair of Vincennes watering-cans said to have been used by Louis XV's mistress were sold on 12 June 1984, one for £29 000, the other for £28 000.

10   Captain Oates' Polar Medal
On 28 June 1984 the medal awarded posthumously after Oates'

self-sacrificing death on Scott's polar expedition of 1912 was
sold for £55 000 – an auction record.

THE DAILY TELEGRAPH INFORMATION SERVICE'S TEN COMMONEST QUESTIONS

The Daily Telegraph Information Service (Tel. 01-353 4242)
will answer enquiries about virtually anything. The ten most
popular subjects are:

Forms of address
The Retail Price
  Index
Company information
Local newspapers
Time differences
Sporting fixtures

Opening times of
  exhibitions and
  stately homes
Spelling and grammar
Biographical
  information
Items in the
  Daily Telegraph

SPECIAL STUDIES

The range of specialist day and evening classes offered to
Londoners is quite remarkable; among those available in
1984/5 were:

Advanced Astrology
Amharic
Anarchism
Badminton for the Deaf
Bangladeshi Games
Christmas Decorations

Hieroglyphic Writing
Kurdish
Occult Studies
Origami
Pigeon-care and
  Breeding

Circus Skills
Corn-dolly Making
Cornish
Extra-sensory
   Perception
Fly-tying

Retreat from Reason
Skiing for the Blind
Storytelling
Tarot
Tibetan
Visual Thinking

TEN UNUSUAL LLOYDS INSURANCE POLICIES

1 A grain of rice with a microscopic portrait of the Queen and the Duke of Edinburgh on it was insured for $20 000.

2 Rudolph Nureyev insured his legs for £190 000.

3 Cutty Sark Whisky offered a £1 million prize to anyone who could capture the Loch Ness Monster alive, and insured against the risk.

4 The American producers of the film *Jonathan Livingston Seagull*, the cast of which was entirely composed of seagulls, insured the lead seagull's life.

5 Forty members of the 'Whiskers Club' of Derbyshire insured their beards for £20 each against fire and theft.

6 Hole-in-one golf insurances are regularly placed – sometimes for as much as $50 000.

7 Composer Richard Stockler insured his ears.

8 A killer whale called 'Namu' was insured for $8000 while it was being towed to Seattle for display in an aquarium.

9 Satellites launched by Comsat, the US Communications

Satellite Corporation, are insured with Lloyds – hence Lloyds' interest in the successful Space Shuttle recovery of two renegade satellites in 1984.

10   The publishers of a book about Princess Anne and Captain Mark Phillips took out a Lloyds policy against the cancellation or postponement of their wedding.

HARRODS' MOST UNUSUAL REQUESTS

Harrods have always claimed to be able to supply anything, as their list of ten unusual requests fulfilled in recent years shows:

1   A Persian rug to Persia.
2   French wine to France.
3   A handkerchief costing 35p to Los Angeles (air freight: £17.50).
4   A replica of a 1901 Ford car to an Arab oil sheik.
5   A fossil excavated in Texas, bought by Harrods and sold to a Texan for re-export to Texas.
6   An elephant bought for Ronald Reagan when he was Governor of California.
7   A gazebo to Saudi Arabia.
8   A skunk ordered by an American (to be sent to his ex-wife).
9   Gooseberries to Saudi Arabia.
10   A refrigerator to Finland.

HARRODS' BESTSELLING ITEMS

The following items account for more than a little of the £200 million in annual sales achieved by Harrods:

1 630 000 packets of Harrods cigarettes @ £1.15 per packet
163 250 PVC bags @ £3.95–£6.50 each
40 000 bottles of Harrods claret @ £3.00 per bottle
19 284 pairs of short cotton socks @ £3.30 a pair
19 000 Harrods model vans @ £3.50 each
2372 Harrods lighters @ £9.50 each
1600 lambswool 'V'-neck pullovers @ £28.00 each
1500 spotted silk ties @ £11.00 each
110 tons of Harrods Christmas pudding @ £2.00 per lb.
75 tons of Harrods sausages @ £1.36 per lb.

THE ORIGINS OF THE NAMES OF TEN WELL-KNOWN LONDON COMPANIES AND PRODUCTS

1 Aquascutum

In 1851 – the year the Great Exhibition was held in London – the Regent Street firm of Bax & Co. patented a rainproof fabric which was subsequently used in the manufacture of raincoats. Seeking a suitably impressive classical name, in 1853 they came up with 'Aquascutum', which is Latin for 'water shield'. The brand name has been in use ever since, and has generated other product names from the same root, such as Eiderscutum and Aquaspectrum.

2 Ascot

Dr Bernard Friedman, a German resident in London, established a company to market gas water heaters manufactured by the German firm of Junkers. In 1933, the year Hitler came to power and when anti-German feeling was growing, Friedman looked for a name that was unmistakably British: the result was 'Ascot'.

3 Biba
The store that represented the 'swinging London' style of the 1960s, and underwent various incarnations in Kensington Church Street and Kensington High Street, got its name from Biruta (whose nickname was Biba), the sister of its founder, entrepreneur Barbara Hulanicki.

4 Bisto
When the gravy powder was introduced in 1910, the advertising slogan that accompanied it was:

> Browns
> I
> Seasons
> Thickens in
> One

Whether the name or the slogan came first is uncertain.

5 Cow Gum
The glue widely used by designers because it has the property of being completely removable without staining or damaging artwork is not, as is popularly thought, made from cows; the firm that makes it was founded in London's Cheapside by Peter Brusey Cow.

6 Cutty Sark
At a lunch given by whisky distillers Berry Bros. & Rudd in their London offices in 1923, guests were invited to suggest a name for a new brand of whisky that the firm planned to export to the USA once Prohibition was repealed. Among those present was the Scottish artist, James McBey, who offered the name 'Cutty Sark'. Not only had the famous tea-clipper bearing this name been in the news on its return to England, but the words had a distinctly Scottish origin, being the name of a kind of shirt worn by a character in Robert Burns' poem, *Tam o'Shanter*. McBey's suggestion was immediately adopted, and he promptly sketched a design for a label featuring the ship with hand-drawn lettering; the printed version

was meant to be a buff colour, but a printer's error made it yellow – and yellow it has remained ever since.

7 His Master's Voice (HMV)

Francis Barraud, a painter of somewhat sentimental subjects, produced a picture of his deceased brother's fox-terrier, Nipper, listening to an Edison phonograph; this he titled, 'His Master's Voice'. In 1899 Barraud decided to paint an updated version of this work, featuring a gramophone horn in place of the old-fashioned phonograph trumpet. He borrowed one from The Gramophone Company, whose managing director, William Barry Owen, offered to buy the painting – provided Barraud agreed to one more alteration: the substitution of an 'Improved Gramophone' for the Edison phonograph. The painting changed hands for £100 and was subsequently used with enormous success as the company's trademark. The original painting is owned by EMI Records and hangs in their London headquarters.

8 Jaeger

Dr Gustav Jaeger wrote a book, *Health Culture*, in which he promoted the notion of health through the wearing of wool and other animal fibres. Lewis Tomalin, a London accountant, was inspired by the book and opened a shop specializing in clothing of this type in Fore Street in February 1884; the sign above the door read, 'Dr Jaeger's Sanitary Woollen System' – and Jaeger became established as the company's name.

9 Liberty

The association of the freedom of the Art Nouveau styles offered by the London firm of Liberty with its name is obvious – but entirely coincidental. The shop in Regent Street was founded in 1875 by Arthur Lasenby Liberty.

10 Three Candlesticks

In the seventeenth century, when there was a shortage of coins, many traders issued their own 'trade coins'. One such token, dated 1649, was discovered in 1799 on the site of the stationers, John Dickinson, in London's Old Bailey. On one side were the initials of the tradesman – 'A.I.K.' – and on the other the legend, 'At the 3 candlesticks', presumably the inn beside which 'A.I.K.' conducted his business. The name was adopted by Dickinson for a range of writing paper that has remained popular since this discovery.

TEN LONDON ROYAL WARRANT HOLDERS

At present a Royal Warrant can be granted by only four members of the Royal Family: the Queen, the Queen Mother, the Duke of Edinburgh and the Prince of Wales. A business may hold warrants from more than one member of the Royal Family, but few hold all four. To become eligible for a Royal Warrant a business must have supplied goods or services to the Royal household for at least three consecutive years.

1 Barrow Hepburn Equipment Ltd, SW8
Manufacturers of Royal Maundy Purses to HM the Queen
A curious mixture of the practical and the ceremonial: Barrow Hepburn's main business is in industrial safety harnesses, but they also make the red and white leather purses in which the Queen distributes the traditional 'Maundy money'.

2 Edwardes (Camberwell) Ltd, SE5
Suppliers of Mopeds to HM the Queen
Edwardes have been supplying the orderlies at Buckingham Palace with mopeds for over fifteen years. Opened in 1908 by the present Mr Edwardes' grandfather, the shop sells bicycles, mopeds and motorcycles.

3 Hatchards Ltd, W1
Booksellers to HM the Queen, HM the Queen Mother, HRH the Duke of Edinburgh and HRH the Prince of Wales
The Royal Family are not noted frequenters of bookshops and Hatchards is the only one in London to hold a Royal Warrant – but it does hold all four.

4 James Lock & Co. Ltd, SW1
Hatters to HRH the Duke of Edinburgh
Founded in 1676, Locks (with Garrards, the Crown Jewellers), remodelled the Imperial State Crown for the Queen's coronation and recently supplied the Princess of Wales with a riding hat.

5 Mayfair Window Cleaning Co. Ltd, SW8
Window Cleaners to HM the Queen Mother
It takes four Mayfair Window Cleaning men one day to clean the windows at Clarence House, the Queen Mother's London residence. Since the company started in 1910, they have cleaned windows for the Prince of Wales (later Edward VII) and, since 1959, for the Queen Mother.

6 Rigby & Peller, W1
Corsetières to HM the Queen
The most intimate service for which a Royal Warrant has been granted. They have held it since 1960.

7 Stephens Brothers Ltd, W1
Shirtmaker and Hosier to HRH the Duke of Edinburgh
Awarded their first Royal Warrant by George VI in 1938 as Hosiers, other fans of their knee-length socks have included Lord Mountbatten and the Duke of Edinburgh. Unfortunately, their socks are not available to the public, although their shirts are.

8 Truefitt & Hill, W1
Hairdressers to HRH the Duke of Edinburgh
First appointed Wigmaker to George IV, their most distinguished customer is the Duke of Edinburgh. They used to cut the Prince of Wales' hair too, but since his marriage he has been using Princess Diana's hairdresser.

9 R. Twining & Co. Ltd, WC2
Tea and Coffee Merchants to HM the Queen
Even if you are lucky enough to be invited to a Royal garden party, you won't be drinking the tea drunk in the Royal drawing rooms – though it may well be tea from Twinings. The

company was granted its first Royal Warrant by Queen Victoria.

10 Wilkinson Sword Ltd, W3
Sword Cutlers to H M the Queen
Famed for their razor blades, Wilkinson Sword have been
Royal sword manufacturers since the reign of Queen Victoria.
If you are knighted, it will be with a Wilkinson sword.

[List specially prepared for *The Londoner's Almanac* by Nina Grunfeld, author of *The
Royal Shopping Guide* (Pan Books, 1984).]

TEN VANISHED DEPARTMENT
STORE NAMES

1 Bon Marché
Britain's first purpose-built department store was established
in Brixton Road in 1877. It was converted into a market after
the Second World War, but was eventually compelled to close.

2 Bourne & Hollingsworth
One of the most recent casualties, Bourne & Hollingsworth
was established in 1894 and had been at its Oxford Street site
since 1902. It was closed in 1984.

3 Debenham & Freebody
The department store in Wigmore Street grew out of the
expansion of a drapery business dating from the 17th century.
It was closed in 1981.

4 Derry & Toms
The famous Kensington High Street store, expanded from a
mid-19th century fancy goods shop, was closed in 1973. For a
brief period the building was occupied by Biba.

5 A. W. Gamage
Established in 1878, Gamages in Holborn became a major store with one of Britain's leading mail order businesses. It was closed in 1972.

6 Gorringes
Dating from 1858, this Buckingham Palace Road store closed in the 1960s.

7 Marshall & Snellgrove
The name of this notable Oxford Street store, which had been trading since the mid-nineteenth century, disappeared after becoming part of the Debenham Group in 1973.

8 Ponting Bros.
This long-established Kensington High Street store was demolished in 1971 although its name lingered as a 'store within a store' in its parent company, Barkers of Kensington.

9 Swan & Edgar
This store had been in business since the early nineteenth century, dominating its Piccadilly Circus site. It was closed in 1982.

10 Whiteley's
This Queensway store went through a dramatic history, which included fires and the murder of its founder, William Whiteley, in 1907. It closed in 1981.

LONDON'S TEN MOST EXPENSIVE ADVERTISING SITES

'Advertising pays.' It also costs. More O'Ferrall operate what are probably the most expensive poster sites in the country, the first two of which work out at £383.56 per day, £15.98 per hour or 26.6p per minute. (The 'L' numbers are their location numbers):

1 L73533V 'Fiat Tower', Great West Road, Hounslow (westbound): £140 000 per year.
2 L73533V 'Fiat Tower', Great West Road, Hounslow (eastbound): £140 000 per year.
3 L6223 West Cromwell Road: £94 680 per year.
4 L3045 West Cromwell Road: £94 680 per year.
5 L3042 West Cromwell Road: £88 740 per year.
6 L3043 West Cromwell Road: £88 740 per year.
7 L3044 West Cromwell Road: £88 740 per year.
8 L6221 West Cromwell Road: £82 920 per year.
9 L6222 West Cromwell Road: £82 920 per year.
10 L6875 West Cromwell Road: £82 500 per year.

THE TWELVE BEST VIEWS IN LONDON

1 Alexandra Palace, Muswell Hill, N22
2 Crystal Palace Park, SE19
3 Hampstead Heath, NW3
4 Highgate Archway (the bridge over Archway Road), N6
5 London Hilton Hotel roof restaurant, 22 Park Lane, W1
6 The Monument, EC2
7 National Westminster Tower, Old Broad Street, EC2
8 New Zealand House, Martini Terrace, Haymarket, SW1
9 Primrose Hill, NW3 and NW8
10 Royal Observatory, Greenwich Park, SE10
11 St Paul's Cathedral, EC4
12 Westminster Cathedral, Francis Street, SW1

LONDON'S TEN LARGEST PARKS AND OPEN SPACES

PARK	ACREAGE
Epping Forest	6000
Richmond Park	2470
Wimbledon Common	1100
Bushy & Hampton Court Park	1099
Hainault Forest	958
Hampstead Heath	800
Regent's Park	487
Coulsdon Commons	430
Trent Park	413
Hyde Park	340

LONDON FARMS

It may come as a surprise to discover that London still has numerous farms. Many are privately owned, but the following are open to the public – though some only to school parties. Phone to check first.

City Farm
232 Grafton Road, NW5   01-482 2861
Pigs and other animals – and near the City Farms Advisory Service, 15 Wilkin Street, NW5 Tel 01-267 9421, which supplies information on London's farms.

Deen Farm
Batsworth Road, Mitcham   01-648 1461
About 1 acre, with horses, ponies, chickens, ducks, rabbits, geese, guinea fowl, pigs, sheep and goats.

Elm Farm
Gladstone Terrace, SW8   01-627 1130
Around .75 acre beside railway tracks, with horses, goats, poultry and ducks.

Mudchute Community Farm
Manchester Road, E14   01-515 5901
The largest community farm in London – 30 acres with horses, ponies, cows, sheep, goats, pigs, chickens, ducks and rabbits.

Spitalfields Community Farm
Buxton Street, E1   01-247 8762
Various animals in another unlikely location.

Stepping Stones
c/o Dame Colet House, Ben Jonson Road, E1   01-790 8204
4.5 acres with cows, bullocks, pigs, goats, sheep, pony, poultry, rabbits and guinea pigs.

Surrey Docks Farm
Gulliver Street, SE16   01-231 1010
Covering 1.5 acres, it has goats, chickens, donkeys, pigs, ducks, geese and bees.

Vauxhall City Farm
24 St Oswald's Place, SE11   01-582 4204
1 acre, with goats, pigs, ponies, donkeys, chickens, ducks, geese, sheep, rabbits, guinea pigs and ferrets.

The following are owned by the GLC and are available for visits by ILEA schools and occasionally by the public (GLC Department for Recreation and the Arts, 91–95 Uxbridge Road, W5 5JT Tel: 01-579 0011 for further information).

Park Lodge Farm, Harefield
Whiteheath Farm, Harefield
Bourne Farm, Harefield
Dyrham Park Farm, Potters Bar
North Lodge Farm, Enfield

AVERAGE TEMPERATURES IN LONDON, 1961–1980

[In degrees Centigrade]

Maximum

Jan	Feb	Mar	Apr	May	Jun
7.2	7.9	10.2	13.0	16.7	20.1

Jul	Aug	Sep	Oct	Nov	Dec	Year
21.6	21.4	19.1	15.5	10.6	8.0	14.3

Mean

Jan	Feb	Mar	Apr	May	Jun
5.4	5.7	7.3	9.7	13.0	16.1

Jul	Aug	Sep	Oct	Nov	Dec	Year
17.9	17.7	15.7	12.7	8.5	6.2	11.3

Minimum

Jan	Feb	Mar	Apr	May	Jun
3.6	3.6	4.5	6.4	9.3	12.2

Jul	Aug	Sep	Oct	Nov	Dec	Year
14.2	14.0	12.3	10.0	6.3	4.4	8.4

MINIMUM TEMPERATURES IN LONDON, 1961–1980

[In degrees Centigrade; D = Day; N = Night]

MONTH	DATE/YEAR	TEMP
January	D:25/63	−2.2
	N:25/63	−6.9
February	D:02/63	−1.8
	N:02/63	−6.0
March	D:06/71	−0.1
	N:03/65	−3.8

April	D:14/66	1.8
	N:11/78	−0.7
May	D:01/79	8.0
	N:02/79	1.6
June	D:01/61	10.7
	N:01/62	4.2
July	D:04/62 and 01/80	13.9
	N:04/65	8.6
August	D:31/78	14.1
	N:01/65	9.2
September	D:14/75	10.3
	N:22/79	5.2
October	D:30/74	6.9
	N:31/74	2.1
November	D:16/65	2.0
	N:15/65	−2.9
December	D:31/78	−1.9
	N:24/63	−6.9

MAXIMUM TEMPERATURES IN LONDON, 1961–1980

[In degrees Centigrade; D = Day; N = Night]

MONTH	DATE/YEAR	TEMP
January	D:10/71	15.2
	N:15/74	11.4
February	D:14/61	18.5
	N:02/67	11.3
March	D:29/65	23.6
	N:29/68	13.8
April	D:21/68	23.7
	N:20/68	13.5

May	D:07/76	28.4
	N:16/79	16.8
June	D:26/76	34.8
	N:28/76	21.6
July	D:01/61	33.4
	N:02/61	22.3
August	D:07/75	32.3
	N:05/75	20.2
September	D:05/73	30.0
	N:05/73	18.3
October	D:11/78	25.2
	N:10/61	17.2
November	D:10/77	18.2
	N:03/69	14.4
December	D:05/79	15.6
	N:12/61	13.2

EIGHT LONDON WINDMILLS

It is not so long ago that there were many working windmills in London. Great Windmill Street – and, in turn, the Windmill Theatre, in the heart of London's West End – and Millbank were named after mills that were in operation until the eighteenth century. There are still about eight windmills – or vestiges of them – to be seen in the London area:

1 Arkley
Arkley, Hertfordshire
The tower mill, dating from the nineteenth century, was restored in 1930.

2 Brixton
Windmill Gardens, SW2
The windmill was built in 1816 and restored in recent years, but has sadly been repeatedly vandalized.

3 Croydon
John Ruskin School, Upper Shirley Road
A smock mill, it dates from the eighteenth century, but was moved here, probably from an East London location, in about 1857. It was restored in 1962.

4 Plumstead Common
1 Old Mill Road, SE18
The eighteenth-century windmill was converted in the 1840s and is now part of the Old Mill public house.

5 Mitcham Common
Windmill Road, Mitcham, Surrey
Little remains of the post mill dating from 1806. It was struck by lightning in the 1850s and largely dismantled in 1905.

6 Upminster
St Mary's Lane, Upminster, Essex
The 1803 smock mill has been restored to its original condition.

7 Wandsworth Common
Windmill Road, SW18
The small, black mill which still stands, minus its sails, on the Common near Spencer Park was built in 1837 to pump water from the adjacent railway cutting to an artificial lake.

8 Wimbledon Common
Windmill Road, SW19
A unique example of a hollow post-mill built in 1817, and the location of the Wimbledon Windmill Museum.

SEVENTEEN LONDON SUNDIALS

Despite London's reputation for fog and rain, the sun shines often enough for there to have been a demand for sundials.

Many can still be seen around London, among them:

1 Charterhouse, Charterhouse Square, EC1
A 1611 sundial installed when Thomas Sutton established his school and hospital there.

2 Chelsea Embankment and Old Church Street, SW3
Dated 1692, and with a clock next to it, so you can check their respective accuracy.

3 52 Chiswell Street, EC1
With the motto, 'Such is life'.

4 Church of the Holy Sepulchre without Newgate, Holborn Viaduct, EC1
The church was rebuilt after the Great Fire, and the sundial probably dates from c1670.

5 The Dial House, 96B Cornwall Gardens, SW7

6 Essex Court, Middle Temple, EC4
Dated 1685.

7 Inner Temple Gardens, EC4
A kneeling figure of a black man with a sundial on his head by the Dutch sculptor, John Van Nost, was bought in Italy by the Earl of Clare in 1705 and given to Clement's Inn by way of amends for his Indian servant's having killed two of their students.

8 112 Kensington High Street, W8

9 29 Peckham Road, SE5
With the motto, 'Do today's work today'.

10 Pump Court, Middle Temple, EC4
Dating from 1686, with the motto, 'Shadows we are and like shadows depart'.

11   St Clement Danes, Strand, WC2
The sundial on the south side of the tower cost £1.15s.0d. in
1671.

12   St Dunstan in the East, Idol Lane, EC3
A sundial in the garden of the blitzed church commemorates
Hugh Thomson, a former gardener, and is dated 1972.

13   St Katharine Cree, Leadenhall Street, EC3
On the south front, dated 1706, with the motto, 'Not without
light'.

14   Stone Buildings, Lincoln's Inn, WC2
Dated 1794.

15   Sun Alliance Building, Cheapside, EC2
A modern sundial dated 1958, said to be the only accurate
timepiece in Cheapside.

16   Tower Hotel, St Katharine's Way, E1
A modern, 'high tech' sundial.

17   Ye Golden Lion, 51 Dean Street, W1

LONDON'S TEN COMMONEST PLANTS

1   Shepherd's Purse (*Capsella bursa-pastoris*)
2   Chickweed (*Stellaria media*)
3   Bramble (*Rubus ulmifolius*)
4   Hawthorn (*Crataegus monogyna*)
5   White Clover (*Trifolium repens*)
6   Ribwort Plantain (*Plantago lanceolata*)
7   Common Meadow-grass (*Poa annua*)
8   Common Daisy (*Bellis perennis*)

9   Yarrow (*Achillea millefolium*)
10 Dandelion (*Taraxacum officinale*)

THE TEN RAREST ANIMALS AT LONDON ZOO

Species	Estimated numbers in		Numbers in London Zoo
	wild	captivity	
Golden Lion Tamarin	500	300	7
Giant Panda	500–1000	50	2
Lion-tailed Macaque	500	300	3
Przewalski's Wild Horse	<10	500	3
Northern White Rhinoceros	500	16	1
Arabian Oryx	40	300	3
Laysan Duck	50–150	200	2
Hawaiian Goose	c1000	c1000	5
Nduk Eagle Owl	<200	3	3
Chinese Alligator	500	100	3

[List specially prepared for *The Londoner's Almanac* by Dr B. C. R. Bertram, Curator of Mammals, The Zoological Society of London.]

LONDON ZOO ADOPTION CHARGES

In 1982 London Zoo inaugurated a successful scheme whereby individuals (or schools, companies or other organizations) can buy £10 or £30 'adoption units' and thereby pay part or all of the costs of upkeep of a chosen animal for a year. By paying for one £30 unit you can thus, for example, cover the costs of feeding and caring for a whole parrot or 1/166th of an elephant. Contact the Adoption Office at the Zoo (Tel: 01-722 3333) if you are interested in adopting an animal. The following is a list of costs per animal per year:

£10

Rock cavy	Quail	Honeycreeper
Shrew	Pheasant	Lizard
Dwarf/Chinese hamster	Dove	Fish
	Pigeon	Insect
Nile rat	Weaver	

£30

Sugar glider	Chinchilla	Snake
Fruit bat	Fat dormouse	Parrot
Squirrel	Cockatiel	

£60

Lemur	Tamarin	Large snake
Douroucouli	Woodchuck	Mouflon
Marmoset	Porcupine	Barbary sheep

£90

Echidna	Ring-tailed coati	Flamingo
Saki monkey		Small bird of prey
Ring-tailed lemur	Mongoose	Owl
	Wild boar	Crane

£150

Kangaroo	Diana monkey	Blackbuck
Pig-tailed macaque	Lar gibbon	Eagle

£250

Hog badger	Emu	Crocodile
Llama	Penguin	

£350

Addax	Pelican
Ostrich	Giant anteater

£500

Grey wolf	Aardvark	Chimpanzee
Cheetah	Greater kudu	

£750

Orang-utan	Puma	Pygmy hippo
Gorilla	Zebra	Reindeer

£1000

Leopard	Asiatic black bear	American black bear
Jaguar		Sloth bear

£1500

Brown bear	Black rhino	Gaur
Lion	Giraffe	American bison
Tiger		

£2000

Californian sealion
White rhino

£4000

Polar bear
Giant panda

£3000

Okapi

£5000

Elephant

CRUFT'S DOG SHOW WINNERS

Charles Cruft (1846–1938) held his first dog show in West-minster in 1886. It was called 'Cruft's Dog Show' from 1891 and is now held at Olympia under the auspices of the Kennel Club. The award for 'Best in Show' was introduced in 1928.

YEAR	BREED	NAME	OWNER
1928	Greyhound	Primely Sceptre	H. Whitley
1929	Scottish Terrier	Heather Necessity	E. Chapman
1930	Spaniel (Cocker)	Luckystar of Ware	H. S. Lloyd
1931	Spaniel (Cocker)	Luckystar of Ware	H. S. Lloyd
1932	Retriever (Labrador)	Bramshaw Bob	Lorna, Countess Howe
1933	Retriever (Labrador)	Bramshaw Bob	Lorna, Countess Howe
1934	Greyhound	Southball Moonstone	B. Hartland Worden
1935	Pointer	Pennine Prima Donna	A. Eggleston
1936	Chow Chow	Ch Choonam Hung Kwong	Mrs V. A. M. Mannooch
1937	Retriever (Labrador)	Ch Cheveralla Ben of Banchory	Lorna, Countess Howe
1938	Spaniel (Cocker)	Exquisite Model of Ware	H. S. Lloyd
1939	Spaniel (Cocker)	Exquisite Model of Ware	H. S. Lloyd
1940–47	(no show held in war period)		
1948	Spaniel (Cocker)	Tracy Witch of Ware	H. S. Lloyd
1949	(Cancelled due to outbreak of Foot and Mouth disease)		

1950	Spaniel (Cocker)	Tracy Witch of Ware	H. S. Lloyd
1951	Welsh Terrier	Twynstar Dyma-fi	Capt & Mrs I. M. Thomas
1952	Bulldog	Ch Noways Chuckles	J. T. Barnard
1953	Great Dane	Ch Elch Elder of Ouborough	W. G. Siggers
1954	(Cancelled due to industrial action)		
1955	Poodle (Standard)	Ch Tzigane Aggri of Nashend	Mrs A. Proctor
1956	Greyhound	Treetops Golden Falcon	Mrs W. de Casembroot and Miss H. Greenish
1957	Keeshond	Ch Vollrijk of Vorden	Mrs I. M. Tucker
1958	Pointer	Ch Chiming Bells	Mrs W. Parkinson
1959	Welsh Terrier	Ch Sandstorm Saracen	Mesdames Leach and Thomas
1960	Irish Wolfhound	Sulhamstead Merman	Mrs Nagle and Miss Clark
1961	Airedale Terrier	Ch Riverina Tweedsbairn	Mrs P. McCaughey and Mrs D. Schuth
1962	Fox Terrier (Wire)	Ch Crackwyn Cockspur	H. L. Gill
1963	Lakeland Terrier	Rogerholm Recruit	W. Rogers
1964	English Setter	Sh Ch Silbury Soames of Madavale	Mrs A. Williams
1965	Alsatian (GSD)	Ch Fenton of Kentwood	Miss S. H. Godden
1966	Poodle (Toy)	Oakington Puckshill Amber Sunblush	Mrs C. E. Perry

1967	Lakeland Terrier	Ch Stingray of Derryabah	Mr and Mrs W. Postlewaite
1968	Dalmatian	Ch Fanhill Faune	Mrs J. Woodyatt
1969	Alsatian (GSD)	Ch Hendrawen's Nibelung of Charavigne	Mr and Mrs E. J. White
1970	Pyrenean Mountain Dog	Bergerie Knur	Mr and Mrs F. S. Prince
1971	Alsatian (GSD)	Ch Ramacon Swashbuckler	Prince Ahmed Husain
1972	Bull Terrier	Ch Abraxas Audacity	Miss V. Drummond-Dick
1973	Cavalier King Charles Spaniel	Alansmere Aquarius	Messrs Hall and Evans
1974	St Bernard	Ch Burtonswood Bossy Boots	Miss M. Hindes
1975	Fox Terrier (Wire)	Ch Brookewire Brandy of Layven	Messrs Benelli and Dondina
1976	West Highland White Terrier	Ch Dianthus Buttons	Mrs K. Newstead
1977	English Setter	Bournehouse Dancing Master	Mr G. F. Williams
1978	Fox Terrier (Wire)	Ch Harrowhill Huntsman	Miss E. Howles
1979	Kerry Blue Terrier	Eng Am Ch Callaghan of Leander	Mrs W. Streatfield

1980	Retriever (Flat-coated)	Ch Shargleam Blackcap	Miss P. Chapman
1981	Irish Setter	Ch Astley's Portia of Rua	Miss C. M. H. and Mrs M. E. P. Tuite
1982	Poodle (Toy)	Ch Grayco Hazelnut	Mrs L. A. Howard
1983	Afghan Hound	Ch Montravia Kaskarak Hitari	Mrs P. Gibbs
1984	Lhasa Apso	Ch Saxon Springs Hackensack	Mrs J. Blyth
1985	Poodle (Standard)	Ch Montravia Tommy-Gun	Miss M. Gibbs

TEN ANIMALS THAT ACHIEVED FAME IN LONDON

1 Chance

Chance, a bull terrier-mastiff cross, attached himself to the Chandos Street fire station in the 1870s and soon proved his worth by detecting a girl overcome by smoke – an act witnessed by the Prince of Wales, a keen amateur fireman. He accompanied numerous calls and was said to be able to recognize false alarms. In 1882 he was fatally injured by a collapsing wall at a blazing printing works; his body was stuffed, put in a glass case and used to raise money – a total of £123 10s 9d – for the family of a dead fireman's family. It is said that his ghostly form was later seen in the flames of burning buildings.

2 Chi-Chi

The giant panda Chi-Chi was acquired by London Zoo in 1958 and became an immediate favourite. Her stardom was increased when she was flown to Moscow in an attempt to mate her with An-An, although this and a subsequent wooing in 1968, when An-An visited London, proved unsuccessful. Chi-Chi died in 1972, but was replaced in 1974 by the Chinese who presented the Zoo with Ching-Ching, a female, and Chia-Chia, a male – and the father (by artificial insemination) of the only giant panda born in Europe, at Madrid Zoo.

3 Dash
Queen Victoria's favourite pet, a King Charles spaniel she had from the time she was a Princess, was frequently referred to in her journals and letters – with a good deal more affection than she showed for many people – as 'Dashy'.

4 Flush
Elizabeth Barrett Browning's dog was immortalized in her poetry, and is the subject of Virginia Woolf's *Flush: A Biography* (1933).

5 Guy
The enormously popular gorilla at London Zoo joined the Zoo on Guy Fawkes Day, 5 November 1947, hence his name – which was doubly appropriate as he was brought to England by a superintendent of the Paris Zoo, a M. Foulkes. Guy drew huge crowds – there were even stories of people spending a fortnight's holiday in the Zoo just to be near him. After his death on 8 June 1978, his body was presented to the Natural History Museum. There is also a statue of him at Crystal Palace Park by David Wynne, set up in 1962, and one at the Zoo by William Timym, unveiled in 1982.

6 Jumbo
The first African elephant in England, Jumbo was acquired by London Zoo in 1865 and for many years was one of the Zoo's most popular animals. He became dangerous and in 1882, despite public protests, was sold for £2000 to the American showman Phineas T. Barnum, and shipped to the USA. Jumbo, who gave his name to anything huge, was killed by a train in 1885.

7 Kaspar

Kaspar, 'the Savoy cat', is a model made by Basil Ionides, who is seated at any dinner party for thirteen at the Savoy Hotel. He is given a napkin, cutlery and a complete meal. He has been kidnapped (or catnapped?) more than once, and was a great favourite of Winston Churchill whenever he dined there.

8 Sefton

The horse that, though injured, survived the IRA bombing of the Household Cavalry in Hyde Park in 1983, became a national hero and symbol of indomitable courage in the face of terrorism.

9 Tim

Known as 'the Paddington dog', a mongrel called Tim used to meet trains arriving at Paddington with a collecting box for a railway workers' widows and orphans fund round his neck. After his death in 1902 his stuffed body continued to perform the same charitable service.

10 Dick Whittington's cat

The anonymous hero of pantomime, whose statue can be seen at the bottom of Highgate, where Richard Whittington is alleged to have heard the bells that urged him to return to London to become Lord Mayor. Whittington – who really existed – paid for the rebuilding of the church of St Michael Paternoster Royal and is commemorated in the stained glass there; coincidentally, during renovations, a mummified cat was found in the church.

THE COMMONEST BIRDS IN LONDON

Feral pigeon	Wren	Robin
Wood pigeon	Songthrush	Dunnock
Blue tit	Blackbird	Starling

THE RAREST BIRDS IN LONDON

	*No. of sightings since 1900**
Squacco Heron	1
Black Kite	2
Baird's Sandpiper	3
Red-throated Pipit	3
Serin	3
Buff-breasted Sandpiper	4
Caspian Tern	4
Crane	4
Red-rumped Swallow	5
Alpine Swift	10
Dipper	11
Bluethroat	11

* in a 20 mile radius from St Paul's

[*Source:* The London Natural History Society *The London Bird Report* 1982.]

TEN LONDON DRINKING FOUNTAINS

The Metropolitan Free Drinking Fountain Association was established in 1859 to supply drinking water, particularly in poor areas of London, in order to overcome shortages, cholera and intemperance. By 1861 they had opened 85 fountains, and 594 by 1886. Their fountains, and those of other charitable organizations, can still be seen throughout London, including:

1 Church of the Holy Sepulchre without Newgate, Holborn Viaduct, EC1
The Association's first drinking fountain, opened on 21 April 1859, once used by 6000 people a day.

2 Lincoln's Inn Fields, WC2
A white stone and marble fountain erected in the north-west corner in 1861, with the inscription, 'The Fear of the Lord is the Fountain of Life'.

3 Victoria Tower Gardens, SW1
Set up in 1865 in Great George Street, SW1, later moved to this site, it has four large polished bowls under a 30ft gothic canopy. It is a memorial to Sir Thomas Fowell Buxton, a social reformer.

4 Clapham Common, SW4
Sir Charles Barry's *Woman of Samaria* fountain (1884) on the north side depicts a woman offering water to an aged cripple. It originally stood by London Bridge, but was moved here in 1894.

5 Victoria Park, E9
The elaborate gothic drinking fountain standing 58.5ft high was presented by Angela Burdett-Coutts and cost nearly £6000. It was unveiled in 1862 before a crowd of 10000.

6 Marlborough Gate, Kensington Gardens, W2
The fountain was installed in 1939 to mark the 80th anniversary of the Association. It comprises a stone bowl on a pedestal crowned by a bronze of two wrestling bears.

7 Grosvenor Gate, Hyde Park, W1
The gothic fountain was a gift in 1863 of Maharaja Meerza Vijiaran Gajapatiran Manea Sooltan Bhandoor of Vijianagram.

8 Royal Exchange, EC3

Made by J. Whitehead, it depicts a bronze maiden beneath a four-columned Ionic canopy.

9 Broad Walk, Regent's Park, NW1

The 1881 fountain comprises a classical female figure with two swans.

10 Trafalgar Square, WC2

On both the east and west walls are fountains given by the Association in 1960.

TEN LONDON RIVERS AND CANALS

1 The River Fleet

Flowing from Highgate to the Thames via Camden Town and the City, the Fleet was used by boats as early as the twelfth century. In 1670 it was rebuilt as a proper navigation, with wharves on each bank as far as Holborn. During the eighteenth century the river was arched over, and the Fleet Market took place on top of it. Later still it became a sewer and storm drain, now hidden beneath Farringdon Street.

2 The Kensington Canal

In 1824 a canal was cut from Chelsea to Warwick Road, near Olympia, to encourage the development of Kensington. The section from Olympia to the King's Road was closed in 1859, but the remainder continued in use, with a large dock complex on the Thames near Lots Road Power Station. Until the canal's final closure in 1959, it was still possible to visit the King's Road by boat.

3 The Grosvenor Canal

Built originally to connect Chelsea Waterworks to the Thames, the Grosvenor became a canal in 1823 and operated for many years carrying coal to Pimlico. In 1859 the building of Victoria Station obliterated most of the Canal, and the remainder progressively shortened over the years. Today 163 yards of canal survives, linked to the Thames by a smart lock north-east of Chelsea Bridge, and regularly used by Westminster Council's refuse barges.

4 The Romford Canal

Work started in 1877 on this unlikely waterway, planned to link Romford to the Thames. Work stopped the same year, and was never resumed. However, a length of canal, complete with lock, but going nowhere, still survives in Dagenham, near the A13.

5 The Grand Surrey Canal

Opened in 1810 from the Thames at Rotherhithe to Camberwell, the Grand Surrey never lived up to its name, even though a branch to Peckham was added in 1826. In 1864 the Canal became part of the Surrey Docks complex, and remained in use up to the 1940s. Parts survived until the closure of the Surrey Docks in 1970, and can still be traced, for example the section crossed by the Old Kent Road.

6 The Croydon Canal

Opened in 1809, the Croydon Canal ran from New Cross, where it met the Grand Surrey Canal, to Croydon, a difficult 9-mile route that included 26 locks. Never successful, it was closed in 1836 and turned into a railway – its final gesture being to burst its banks and flood 200 houses in Deptford. A short section survives in Anerley, converted into a park.

7 The Thames and Medway Canal

This unusual canal was built in 1824 at enormous cost to link the two rivers, and thus allow barges to avoid the passage round the North Foreland. It was seven miles long, over 2.5 of which were through the huge Strood Tunnel – the second longest canal tunnel ever built in England. Regular cargoes of fruit and hops were carried along it until 1845 when a railway was built alongside it and through the Tunnel. A section north of the Tunnel survived in use until the 1930s and this can still be traced. The Tunnel can be seen by taking the train from Gravesend to Strood.

8 The River Lee
Navigable since the 1820s from Hertford to the Thames at Limehouse, the Lee is a river of considerable character. Heavily industrialized from Enfield southwards through East London, the upper reaches of it are by contrast rural and attractive. Much of the Lee is now part of a large Regional Park, enjoyably explored by foot or by boat and easily accessible.

9 The Regent's Canal
Opened in 1820 to link the Grand Union Canal with the Thames and docks, the Regent's Canal runs from Paddington to Limehouse. Its route, a contrasting blend of elegance and decay, includes Little Venice, Regent's Park and the Zoo, Camden Town, St Pancras, Islington and Hackney. There are two tunnels, twelve locks and many unexpected views of London's backdoors. Water buses and towpath walks make it one of London's easiest waterways to explore.

10 The Paddington Arm of the Grand Union
The Grand Union Canal, the main waterway link between London and the Midlands, joins the Thames at Brentford. A long branch leads eastwards to Paddington, to meet the Regent's Canal at Little Venice. Opened in 1801, it played a large part in the development of west London. Its course is through a mixture of industry and suburbia, but there are some unexpected treats, for example Kensal Green Cemetery and a 1930s concrete aqueduct carrying the Canal over the North Circular Road at Alperton. This canal, the Regent's Canal and the Thames offer an unusual circular tour of London by water for boat-owners with a weekend to spare.

[Apart from using a boat or walking along the towpaths, one of the best ways to explore canals is by bicycle. It is necessary, however, to obtain a licence from the British Waterways Board Engineering Department, Tel: 0923 31363.]

[List specially prepared for *The Londoner's Almanac* by Paul Atterbury, author of *Nicholson's Guides to the Waterways of Britain* (Nicholson, 1969–73) and *English Rivers and Canals* (Weidenfeld & Nicolson, 1984).]

REACHES OF THE THAMES

For many centuries, various sections, or 'reaches' of the Thames have had names. From the estuary to Kew, these are:

Sea
 Gravesend
  Northfleet Hope
   St Clement's or Fiddlers'
    Long
     Erith Rands
      Erith
       Halfway
        Barking
         Gallions
          Woolwich
           Bugsby's
            Blackwall
             Greenwich
              Limehouse
               Lower Pool
                Upper Pool
                 London Bridge
                  Unnamed (London Bridge
                  to Westminster Bridge)
                   Unnamed (Westminster
                   Bridge to Vauxhall Bridge)
                    Nine Elms
                     Chelsea
                      Battersea
                       Wandsworth
                        Barn Elms
                         Chiswick
                          Corney
                           Mortlake

TEN SHIPS MOORED PERMANENTLY ON THE THAMES

1 HMS *Belfast*, Symon's Wharf, Nive Lane, SE1
The Royal Navy's largest cruiser. Open to the public.

2 HMS *Chrysanthemum*, King's Reach, Victoria Embankment, EC4
A First World War sloop – with HMS *Wellington*, the London HQ of the Royal Naval Reserve. Not open to the public.

3 The *Cutty Sark*, King William Walk, Greenwich, SE10
The famous nineteenth-century tea-clipper now in dry dock. Open to the public.

4 RRS *Discovery*, St Katharine's Dock, E1
The ship in which Captain Robert Falcon Scott sailed on his ill-fated voyage to the Antarctic. Now one of several vessels in St Katharine's Dock opened to the public by the Maritime Trust.

5 *Gipsy Moth IV*, King William Walk, Greenwich, SE10
The boat in which Sir Francis Chichester circumnavigated the world (1966–67). Open to the public.

6 *Hispaniola*, Victoria Embankment, WC2
A floating restaurant.

7 HMS *President*, King's Reach, Victoria Embankment, EC4
With HMS *Chrysanthemum*, the headquarters of the RNR. Not open to the public.

8 *Princess Elizabeth*, Swan Pier, EC4
A paddle steamer with bar and restaurant.

9 PS *Tattershall Castle*, Victoria Embankment, SW1
A floating pub on a former Humber paddle steamer.

10 HMS *Wellington*, King's Reach, Victoria Embankment, EC4
Now serving as the livery hall of the Honourable Company of Master Mariners. Not open to the public.

FISH IN THE THAMES

Improvements in sewage treatment and reduced pollution have resulted in a marked increase in the number of fish in the Thames during the past twenty years. Since 1964 about 110 different species have been recorded in the Thames Estuary (from the tidal limit at Teddington to the mouth – a line between Haven Point in Essex and Warden Point on the Isle of Sheppey in Kent), and over 100 in the formerly heavily polluted stretch between Fulham and Tilbury. The Thames Water Authority is also undertaking an extensive salmon re-stocking programme.

The rarest fish caught in the Thames is probably Eckstrom's Topknot (*Phyrynorhombus regius*), only one example of which has been recorded (at West Thurrock, December 1983). Two examples of the Sea Horse (*Hippocampus ramulosus*) have been caught in recent years (Dagenham, October 1976; West Thurrock, 1982).

The commonest fish in the Inner Estuary, as recorded by the Thames Angling Preservation Society, is the Dace (*Leuciscus leuciscus*). The ten commonest, in descending order, are:

1 Dace	6 Herring
2 Whiting	7 Sprat
3 Sand goby	8 Dover sole
4 Flounder	9 Bib
5 Smelt	10 Bass

The largest fish caught in the Thames in recent times was a 64lb Conger Eel, *Conger conger*, at Erith, December 1977.

Aquatic mammals are also occasionally sighted in the Thames, including a dolphin between Woolwich and Dartford in 1980 and seals at Richmond in 1976 and 1977 and at Blackfriars, 1978.

THAMES BRIDGES AND TUNNELS

CROSSING	DATE	NOTES
Gallions Reach		Proposed road tunnel
Woolwich Subway	1876	Pedestrians only
Blackwall Tunnel	1891–97	Northbound, for pedestrians and vehicles
	1960–67	Southbound
Greenwich Subway	1897–1902	Pedestrians only
Rotherhithe Tunnel	1904–8	Pedestrians and vehicles
Thames Foot Tunnel (Rotherhithe–Wapping)	1825–43	First under-river tunnel
	1866–69	Rebuilt as railway tunnel
	1884	Metropolitan Line
Tower Bridge	1886–94	Pedestrians and vehicles
Tower Subway	1869–70	Pedestrians only (rope-drawn car originally used); redundant 1896; now used for water mains

London Bridge	1stC A D	First wooden bridge
	1176–1209	Stone bridge built
	1823–31	Second stone bridge
	1902–4	Widened
	1967	Sold for £1 million; rebuilt at Lake Havasu, Arizona
	1967–72	Present stone bridge
City and South London Railway Tunnel	1890	First tunnel designed for underground railway; disused 1900
London Bridge – Bank	1900	Northern Line tunnel
Alexandra Bridge	1863–66	Railway bridge to Cannon Street station
	1890s	Widened
Southwark Bridge	1814–19	Pedestrians and vehicles
	1919–21	Replaced
Blackfriars Railway Bridges	1862–64	Western bridge to Ludgate Hill station
	1985	Demolished
	1884–86	Eastern bridge to St Paul's (now Blackfriars) station
Blackfriars Bridge	1760–69	Pedestrians and vehicles
	1860–69	Replaced by present bridge
	1907–10	Widened
Waterloo and City Line	1898	Underground link ('The Drain')

Waterloo Bridge	1811–17	Pedestrians and vehicles
	1937–42	Replaced by present bridge
Bakerloo Line	1906	
Northern Line	1926	
Hungerford Bridge	1841–45	Pedestrian bridge
	1860–64	Rebuilt as railway and footbridge
	1900	Enlarged
Westminster Bridge	1738–50	Pedestrians and vehicles
	1854–62	Replaced by present bridge
Lambeth Bridge	1861–62	Pedestrians and vehicles
	1929–32	Replaced by present bridge
Vauxhall Bridge	1811–16	Pedestrians and vehicles
	1881	Two central piers removed
	1895– 1906	Replaced by present bridge
Victoria Line	1971	
Grosvenor Bridge	1858–60	Railway bridge to Victoria
	1865–67	Widened
	1907	Widened
	1963–67	Rebuilt
Chelsea Bridge	1851–58	Pedestrians and vehicles
	1936–37	Replaced by present bridge

Albert Bridge	1871–73	Pedestrians and vehicles
	1884	Strengthened
	1971–73	Central piers added
Battersea Bridge	1771–72	Pedestrians only
	1886–90	Replaced by present bridge for pedestrians and vehicles
Battersea Railway Bridge	1861–63	
Wandsworth Bridge	1870–73	Pedestrians and vehicles
	1936–40	Replaced by present bridge
Putney Railway Bridge	1887–89	
Putney Bridge	1727–29	Pedestrians and vehicles
	1871–72	Modified
	1882–86	Replaced by present bridge
Hammersmith Bridge	1824–27	Pedestrians and perhaps vehicles
	1883–87	Replaced by present bridge
	1973–76	Strengthened
Barnes Railway and Footbridge	1846–49	
	1891–95	Reconstructed
Chiswick Bridge	1933	Pedestrians and vehicles
Kew Railway Bridge	1864–69	

Kew Bridge	1758–59	Timber bridge for pedestrians and vehicles
	1784–89	Replaced by stone bridge
	1903	Rebuilt
Richmond Lock and Footbridge	1894	Pedestrians only
Twickenham Bridge	1931–33	Pedestrians and vehicles
Richmond Railway Bridge	1848	
	1906–8	Reconstructed
Richmond Bridge	1774–77	Pedestrians and vehicles
	1937–39	Widened
Teddington Footbridge	1888–89	Pedestrians only
Kingston Railway Bridge	1860–63	
	1907	Replaced
Kingston Bridge	Medieval	
	1825–28	Replaced by present bridge for pedestrians and vehicles
	1914	Widened
Hampton Court Bridge	1751–53	First bridge
	1778	Rebuilt
	1865	Replaced by iron bridge
	1930–33	Replaced by present bridge for pedestrians and vehicles

THE ALBERT MEMORIAL: 169 VICTORIAN ART HEROES

The Albert Memorial in Kensington Gardens is one of London's most remarkable monuments – not only to the Prince Consort, but also to the arts and crafts of the Victorian age. In addition to the massive bronze statue of Albert, figures representing 'Christian and Moral Virtues' and groups depicting 'Skills' (Agriculture, Manufactures, Commerce and Engineering) and 'The Continents' (Europe, Asia, Africa and America), there is an extraordinary portrait gallery of 169 artistic heroes of the day. Grouped by vocation and country of origin, they form a continuous frieze of full-length figures round the entire base of the Memorial. Not only was this one of the most ambitious sculpture projects ever undertaken, but in the choice of subjects we have a record in stone of the men the Victorian artistic establishment regarded as the most influential. A century of changing taste later, it is surprising how many important omissions one can spot – and how many Victorian heroes are today all but forgotten.

[Note: The spellings – sometimes idiosyncratic – are as engraved on the frieze.]

POETS AND MUSICIANS

Auber	Moliere	Handel
Mehul	Cervantes	Mozart
Rameau	Virgil	Mendelssohn
Lulli	Dante	Haydn
Gretry	Pythagoras	Weber
Josquin-des-Pres	Homer	Beethoven
Rossini	Chaucer	Tallis
Monteverde	Shakespeare	O. Gibbons
Carissimi	Milton	Lawes
Palestrina	Goethe	Purcell
Guido d'Arezzo	Schiller	Arne
St Ambrose	Bach	Boyce
Corneille	Gluck	Bishop

PAINTERS

Turner	Orcagna	An. Carracci
Wilkie	Giotto	L. Carracci
Reynolds	Fra Angelico	Velasquez
Gainsborough	Ghirlandaio	Murillo
Hogarth	Massacio	Poussin
Rembrandt	da Vinci	Claude
Rubens	Raphael	David
Holbein	Michael Angelo	Gerard
Durer	Bellini	Gericault
H. van Eyck	Titian	Delacroix
J. van Eyck	Mantegna	Vernet
Stephen of	P. Veronese	Delaroche
Cologne	Tintoretto	Ingres
Cimabue	Corregio	Decamps

ARCHITECTS

Pugin	Bramante	Anthemius
Scott	William of	Hermodorus
Cockerell	Wykeham	Apollodorus
Barry	Alberti	Callimachus
Chambers	Brunelleschi	Libon
Vanbrugh	Giotto	Callicrates
Wren	Arnolfo di Lap	Ictinus
Inigo Jones	Erwin von	Mnésikles
Mansart	Steinbach	Chersiphron
Thorpe	Jehan de	Rhoecus
Palladio	Chelles	Metagenes
Vignola	Rob. de Loucy	Theodorus
Delorme	William of Sens	Hiram
Sansovino	William the	Bezaleel
San Gallo	Englishman	Sennacherib
Peruzzi	Abbe Suger	Nitocris
		Cheops

SCULPTORS

Egyptian	Luca della	Bontemps
Assyrian	Robbia	Pilon
Rhoecus	William of	Cano
Dibutades	Ireland	Stone

Bupalus	Verrocchio	Bernini
Phidias	Donatello	Cibber
Scopas	Michael Angelo	Puget
Bryaxis	Torigiano	Gibbons
Praxiteles	Gian. di	Bird
Leochares	Bologna	Bushnell
Lysippus	Bandinelli	Robiliac
Chares	Vischer	Canova
Gilliano di	Cellini	Flaxman
Ravenna	Goujon	David
Niccola Pisano	Baccio	(d'Angers)
Ghiberti	d'Angelo	Thorwaldsen
Torell	Palissy	

SIX GREAT PAINTERS OF LONDON

One notable London picture is given in each case; all major London collections are noted – but they do not contain exclusively London pictures.

1 Canaletto (Giovanni Antonio Canale), 1697–1768
Canaletto first arrived in London in 1746, remaining – with occasional trips to his native Venice – for the next ten years. Although best known for his stunning paintings of Venice, his views of the Thames and Whitehall are outstanding, though as many are in private collections they are less well-known than they might be if hung in a major art gallery.

London: Interior of the Rotunda at Ranelagh, 1754 (National Gallery)
National Gallery, Royal Collection

2 William Hogarth, 1697–1764
Hogarth's series paintings, such as *The Rake's Progress* and *Marriage à la Mode*, are widely known through engravings. Although primarily painted as moral lessons, they also depict many notable eighteenth-century buildings and provide a

vivid impression of London life.

Rake's Progress series (Sir John Soane's Museum)
Coram Foundation, Dulwich Picture Gallery, National Gallery, Royal Collection, Sir John Soane's Museum, Tate Gallery

3 . J. M. W. Turner, 1775–1851
Though a Londoner, Turner only occasionally painted his home town – but his few paintings of London cover dramatic events such as the burning of the Houses of Parliament in 1834.

Moonlight: A Study of Millbank, 1797 (Tate Gallery)
British Museum, Kenwood, National Gallery, Royal Academy, Tate Gallery, Victoria and Albert Museum

4 John Constable, 1776–1837
Constable lived in Charlotte Street, later moving to Hampstead, which he painted several times. His *Opening of Waterloo Bridge, 18 June 1817* was one of his few urban studies.

The Grove, or Admiral's House, Hampstead, c1820 (Tate Gallery)
British Museum, Guildhall Art Gallery, National Gallery, Royal Academy, Tate Gallery, Victoria and Albert Museum

5 Camille Pissarro, 1831–1903
Pissarro, one of the founding fathers of Impressionism, fled France during the Franco–Prussian War of 1870 and stayed in Upper Norwood. His paintings of London include one of Crystal Palace and his well-known *Lordship Lane Station* – formerly believed to depict Penge.

Lordship Lane Station, Lower Norwood, 1871 (Courtauld Institute Galleries)
Courtauld Institute Galleries, National Gallery, Tate Gallery

6 Claude Monet, 1840–1926
Like Pissarro, Monet was an Impressionist refugee who settled in London in 1870, returning in subsequent years to paint various London locations, especially a series of remarkable polychromatic pictures of the Houses of Parliament.

The Thames Below Westminster, 1871 (National Gallery)
Courtauld Institute Galleries, National Gallery, Tate Gallery

AMERICAN PAINTERS IN LONDON

London was once a mecca for American painters, some of whom stayed and became part of the British artistic establishment. Among the most notable are the following. Examples of their works can be seen in the London collections listed – as well as in certain provincial art galleries.

1 Edwin Austin Abbey (1852–1911)
Born in Philadelphia, Abbey visited England in 1878 and settled, occasionally returning to America to undertake murals and other commissions. Apart from his prolific illustrations of Shakespearean themes, he painted the official coronation portrait of Edward VII in 1902. (*Tate Gallery*)

2 Washington Allston (1779–1843)
A student in the studio of Benjamin West, and 'a man of genius and the best painter yet produced by America'., as the poet Coleridge called him. (*National Portrait Gallery*)

3 George Henry Boughton (1883–1905)
Born in England, but grew up in America where he achieved some success as a painter. In about 1862 he returned to London and remained, painting principally subjects drawn from American history. (*Victoria and Albert Museum*)

4 Mather Brown (1761–1831)
Born in Boston, Brown was the first American enrolled in the Royal Academy Schools and became official portrait and historical painter to the Duke of York. (*National Portrait Gallery; Royal Collection*)

5 John Singleton Copley (1738–1815)
Born in Boston, he was encouraged by Benjamin West to move to London where he followed a successful career as a portrait and history painter. (*Courtauld Institute; Guildhall Art Gallery; National Maritime Museum; National Portrait Gallery; Royal Academy; Royal Collection; Tate Gallery; Wellington Museum*)

6 Anna Lea Merritt (1844–1930)
Philadelphia born, she settled in England during the Franco–Prussian War in 1871 and remained for the rest of her life. Her best-known work is *Love Locked Out*. (*Tate Gallery*)

7 John Singer Sargent (1856–1925)
Born in Florence of American parents, he moved from Paris to London where he became the most fashionable portrait painter of his generation. (*National Portrait Gallery; Tate Gallery; Victoria and Albert Museum*)

8 Gilbert Stuart (1755–1828)
From Kingstown, RI, Stuart left for England in 1777 and worked in the studio of Benjamin West. He later returned to America where he was hailed as the greatest portrait painter of the day. (*National Maritime Museum; National Portrait Gallery; Royal Collection; Syon House; Tate Gallery; Victoria and Albert Museum*)

9 Benjamin West (1738–1820)
From his native Springfield, Pa., West travelled to Europe, settling in London in 1863. He rapidly became a favourite royal painter and a founder member and, after Sir Joshua Reynolds, the second President of the Royal Academy. (*Courtauld Institute; National Maritime Museum; National Portrait Gallery; Royal Collection [some on loan to Palace of Westminster]; Royal Academy; Tate Gallery; Victoria and Albert Museum*)

10 James McNeill Whistler (1834–1903)
Whistler was born in Lowell, Mass., and studied art in Paris before settling in London in 1859. Though he was attacked by the critic, John Ruskin, who accused him of 'flinging a pot of paint in the public's face', resulting in a celebrated libel case,

his pioneering work and promotion of Japanese decorative art were hugely influential. (*Courtauld Institute; Tate Gallery; Victoria and Albert Museum*)

THE TEN BEST CONTEMPORARY LONDON MURALS

There are lots of murals in London, some temporary (around building sites for example), many of them permanent but, being the result of some worthy community effort, often poorly executed. The following ten are as permanent as any mural is – i.e.: until the paint falls off. Nine are professional jobs, but the first – of such exceptional charm that it is worth a special visit – is by schoolchildren.

1 Alexandra Park, N10 (in the covered walkway leading from Muswell Hill to The Grove) has a mural by children from the nearby school. It depicts fantastic happenings in the Park.

2 The Royal Oak Murals, W2, underneath the Westway, show heroic workers and were executed by The Public Art Workshop, 1977.

3 Notting Dale Technology Centre, 189–191 Freston Road, W10, has its side (which will be familiar to drivers turning off the A40(M) for Shepherd's Bush) decorated with an appropriately technological mural.

4 The Waterloo Mural (on the station wall by the round-about at the south end of Westminster Bridge) is full of railway-related incident. It is by Caroline Beale and Kate Morris, 1980.

5 The Clerkenwell Mural, by Clarke & Berry, 1983, is behind The Betsy pub at 56 Farringdon Road, EC1, overlooking Farringdon tube station. It contains scenes connected with the locally important printing industry.

6   Maxwell's Restaurant at 17 Russell Street, Covent Garden, WC2, has a wall covered by a Magritte-like extravaganza by Ken White.

7   The Fitzrovia Mural in Tottenham Court Road, W1, near Heals, is a vast conglomeration of local characters and activities. It was painted by Simon Barber and Mike Jones in 1980.

8   The Victorian engineer Brunel's life and times are portrayed in New Cross, SE14, near the railway station. It was painted in 1973 by a group called 'Nine Three Five'.

9   Godwin Court Mural, around the bottom of a large block of flats in Crowndale Road, NW1, is probably London's largest mural. By a team of seven artists, it shows local scenes, especially railways, as befits a mural near both Euston and King's Cross stations.

10   'Wind of Peace' in Creek Road, Greenwich, SE10, near the *Cutty Sark*, shows the locals nonchalantly diverting an attack by huge rockets. It replaced an earlier mural and was completed in 1983 by Greenwich Mural Workshop.

[List specially prepared for *The Londoner's Almanac* by Brian Shuel, a photographer with an interest in murals.]

TEN IMPORTANT LONDON POTTERIES

1   Fulham
The oldest pottery in London, Fulham was established in 1672 on its present site at the western end of the King's Road. Its founder and most famous owner was the stoneware potter John Dwight, whose figures and bottles can be seen in the British Museum. Fulham continued as a typical stoneware pottery

until well into this century, with some decorative art wares being made in the late Victorian period. A small pottery is still in operation at Fulham, and an old bottle oven can still be seen, surrounded by modern development.

2 Chelsea
Established in about 1745 between Lawrence Street and Justice Walk, the Chelsea Porcelain Works quickly gained a reputation for its fine quality and lavishly-coloured wares, based on European and Far Eastern models. Chelsea-made figures, ornaments and tablewares were sold for high prices to leaders of fashion, and Chelsea became the nearest England ever had to a Royal manufactory. In 1769, Chelsea was taken over by the Derby porcelain company and continued to produce florid and extravagant wares until 1784. Nothing of the factory remains.

3 The New Canton Works (Bow)
This, the first custom-built porcelain factory in Britain, opened on Stratford Causeway, east of Bow Bridge, in 1749. Until its closure in 1776 it continued to make figures, tablewares and ornaments in profusion, mostly following European styles and fashions. No trace of the factory remains, but Bow porcelain still excites collectors.

4 Coade
In the 1760s Mrs Eleanor Coade established a factory in Lambeth to make architectural stoneware. Doorways, windows, architectural details, garden ornaments, fireplaces, chimneys, pots and statues were produced in the latest neoclassical styles until the closure of the factory in the 1840s. The site of the factory lies under Waterloo Station, but Mrs Coade's productions can be seen all over London. [See also *The Coade Stone Mystery*, p. 146.]

5 Doulton
During the 18th and 19th centuries the Lambeth waterfront was solid with potteries making domestic stoneware. By the mid 19th century the factory owned by Sir Henry Doulton had become the largest, having swallowed most of its rivals. Its

works, a vast terracotta pile, stretched from Lambeth Bridge to Vauxhall Bridge on the south side of the river and a huge range of domestic and art wares poured from its kilns. In 1956 Doulton closed down in London and moved to Staffordshire, and since then most of the factory has vanished. One decorative terracotta building survives in Black Prince Road, a memorial to this vanished empire and one of London's great forgotten industries.

6 Minton Art Pottery Studio

In 1871 the Minton company, one of Staffordshire's leading potters, opened an art pottery studio in South Kensington. This studio, a joint venture between Minton, the South Kensington Museum (now the Victoria and Albert Museum) and the South Kensington School of Art (now the Royal College of Art) lasted until 1874 when it was closed following a fire. It was a great social success, attracting many artists and students, and introducing many young ladies to the art of pottery decoration, but Minton lost a small fortune in the venture. The site of the studio is now buried beneath the Royal College complex. Largely forgotten today, the studio's main contribution was to launch the Victorian fashion for pictorial and decorative tiles.

7 Martin Brothers

In 1873 the four Martin brothers started a small stoneware pottery in Fulham, which was to produce England's first Studio Pottery. Their creations were individual and bizarre, blending medieval, Renaissance and Japanese ideas. In 1878 they moved to a larger pottery in Southall, and continued to make their unusual wares until the 1920s. Nothing remains of their pottery, but their reputation, as both potters and eccentrics, has grown steadily, and their famous grotesque pottery birds fetch several thousand pounds today. There is a Martinware collection on display in Southall Public Library.

8 William de Morgan

Although best known as a popular novelist and friend of William Morris, William de Morgan spent much of his life making and decorating pottery. Largely self-taught, he concentrated on the decorative styles of Islamic pottery, using bright colours and lustre glazes. Starting with a studio in Chelsea in 1873, he later established a large workshop near Merton where he produced mainly decorative tiles. Always plagued by financial problems, the de Morgan Pottery closed in 1907 and nothing remains today.

9 The Powell Studio

The decorators and designers Alfred and Louise Powell opened a pottery studio in Red Lion Square in 1907. Already associated with the Wedgwood factory, the Powell Studio became for a few years the equivalent of Wedgwood's London branch. Many contemporary artists, such as Sickert, were connected with the studio, while the Powells themselves moved in Bloomsbury circles, and introduced several Bloomsbury artists, including Duncan Grant and Vanessa Bell, to Wedgwood. For some time the Powell Studio acted as a showroom for Wedgwood's more artistic productions and played a major role in the revival of interest in hand-painted decoration during the 1920s and 1930s.

10 Charles Vyse

After working in Staffordshire, Charles Vyse opened a pottery studio with his wife in Cheyne Walk, Chelsea, SW3 in 1919. A great technician and artist, Vyse produced colourful models of London street and market characters as well as fine pottery inspired by Far Eastern styles and traditions until his retirement in 1963. Although little-known, Vyse was a far better potter than many of his more famous contemporaries, such as Bernard Leach.

[List specially prepared for *The Londoner's Almanac* by Paul Atterbury, former Historical Consultant to Royal Doulton and the author of many books on pottery, including *The History of Porcelain* (Orbis, 1980).]

SEVEN TRADITIONAL CRAFTS STILL CARRIED ON IN LONDON

A surprising number of old crafts have either been revived or are still carried out by family firms and individuals in London. Among them are:

1 Barometer glass making
Sinclair, 17 Briset Street, EC1
Make and repair bevelled edged barometer and clock glasses.

2 Boatbuilding
Dave Johnston, Eel Pie Island, Twickenham
Makes boats by traditional methods, including the use of a hand adze.

3 Brushmaking
J. H. Hoolahan Co. Ltd, 748 Enid Street, SE16
Make specialist brooms, including those used for painting lines on football pitches.

4 Cooperage
Young & Co.'s Brewery, Wandsworth High Street, SW18
Make their own barrels for beer which is still delivered on drays drawn by shire horses.

5 Hatmaking
S. Patey (London) Ltd, 1 Amelia Street, SE17
Make traditional hats, including those worn by Beefeaters and Chelsea Pensioners.

6 Ropeworking
Geoffrey Budworth, 45 Stambourne Way, SE19
Makes bellropes and other traditional knotted ropes – and is Hon. Sec. of the International Guild of Knot Tyers.

7 Saddling
W. & H. Gidden Ltd, 112 Tabernacle Street, EC2
Make leather saddles, harnesses and other tack to traditional patterns.

Ten London Customs

Most Londoners make the effort to see the Trooping of the Colour or the Lord Mayor's Show at some time in their lives, but there are many lesser known traditional displays that are still carried out – though their timing should be checked, and some are not open to the public. Among the most interesting are:

1 The Baddeley cake
A cake is cut after the evening show on 6 January at the Drury Lane Theatre. It is paid for from the bequest of Robert Baddeley and enjoyed by the cast of the show; the rest of us, alas, are not allowed in.

2 Beating the bounds
This ceremony is common throughout the country, but one of the most attractive versions takes place at the Tower of London every third Ascension Day. An imposing procession tours the boundary stones which are beaten with willow wands by choir boys.

3 Chinese New Year
Chinese families celebrate for several days, but westerners have to make do with an impressive display of dragons and strange oriental beasts in the streets near Leicester Square on a Sunday afternoon in early February.

4 The clowns' service
A service commemorating the death of the clown Grimaldi is held at Holy Trinity Church, Dalston, at 3.00 p.m. on the first Sunday in February and is attended by many clowns; less amusingly, it is also attended by numerous TV crews and photographers.

5 The costermongers' harvest festival
This is held at 3.00 p.m. on the first Sunday in October at the church of St Martin-in-the-Fields. Most of London's Pearly families gather, and even the vicar wears a pearly surplice.

6 Doggett's coat and badge race

This, the world's oldest rowing race, is held on the Thames from London Bridge to Chelsea, about 1 August, according to the tides. It is for Thames watermen only and the winner receives a huge silver badge and red outfit.

7 Farthing bundles

'Bundles' containing small presents are distributed to children small enough to walk under a special arch, at 10.00 a.m. on the first Saturday of each month at the Fern Street Settlement, E3. Not long ago hundreds would turn up every Saturday; now few children can be bothered.

8 The pancake greaze

This robust custom takes place at Westminster School on Shrove Tuesday. The cook hurls a thick pancake over a bar in the Hall and the boys scramble furiously for it. The one who gets the biggest piece wins a prize.

9 The Vintners' procession

At noon on the second Wednesday in July the Master and Wardens of the Vintners' Company process from Vintners' Hall to St James, Garlickhythe, carrying nosegays, preceded by porters sweeping the way clean with brooms.

10 The widow's bun

At lunchtime on Good Friday at The Widow's Son in Devons Road, E3, a fresh hot cross bun is added, by a sailor, to the large collection awaiting the return of the widow's long-lost son.

[List specially prepared for *The Londoner's Almanac* by Brian Shuel who has been studying and photographing folk customs for over twenty years and is the author/photographer of the forthcoming *National Trust Book of British Customs* (Webb and Bower).]

London's Twenty-five Oldest Clubs

CLUB	FOUNDED	CLUB	FOUNDED
White's	1693	East India	1849
Boodle's	1762	Savage	1857
Brooks's	1764	Arts	1863
MCC	1787	Junior Carlton	1864
Travellers'	1819	Naval and	1864
Athenaeum	1824	Military	
Oriental	1824	Turf	1868
Garrick	1831	Savile	1868
City of London	1832	National	1882
Reform	1832	Liberal	
Carlton	1832	Eccentric	1890
Army and Navy	1837	Chelsea Arts	1891
Conservative	1840	Royal	1897
Gresham	1843	Automobile	

The Livery Companies of the City of London

The livery companies grew out of the city craft guilds of the fourteenth century, but today they function more as charitable, educational and social institutions than as trade associations. At one time all had halls and often extensive grounds, but as companies such as the Bonnet Makers, Virginals Makers and Heumers (helmet makers) were disbanded or absorbed and buildings were destroyed or sold to raise funds, the number of halls has dwindled to 35. Today the liverymen elect the sheriffs of London and the Lord Mayor. In the time of Henry VIII, long and bitter disputes over the rank of the various livery companies were resolved when their governing body, the Court of Aldermen, established a list in order of precedence, headed by the so-called 'Great Twelve'. Although companies have left and joined, and some have not yet been granted official livery, this list has remained in the same order ever since.

List of livery companies in numerical order of precedence
(* = companies with livery halls)

*1	Mercers	31	Plumbers
*2	Grocers	*32	Innholders
*3	Drapers	*33	Founders
*4	Fishmongers	34	Poulters
*5	Goldsmiths	35	Cooks
*6	Skinners	*36	Coopers
*7	Merchant Taylors	37	Tylers and Bricklayers
*8	Haberdashers	38	Bowyers
*9	Salters	39	Fletchers
*10	Ironmongers	40	Blacksmiths
*11	Vintners	41	Joiners
*12	Clothworkers	42	Weavers
*13	Dyers	43	Woolmen
*14	Brewers	44	Scriveners
*15	Leathersellers	45	Fruiterers
*16	Pewterers	*46	Plaisterers
*17	Barbers	*47	Stationers and Newspaper Makers
*18	Cutlers		
*19	Bakers		
*20	Wax Chandlers	48	Broderers
*21	Tallow Chandlers	49	Upholders
		50	Musicians
*22	Armourers and Braziers	51	Turners
		52	Basketmakers
*23	Girdlers	*53	Glaziers (*hall shared with 84*)
*24	Butchers		
*25	Saddlers	54	Horners
*26	Carpenters	55	Farriers
27	Cordwainers	56	Paviors
*28	Painters	57	Loriners
29	Curriers	*58	Apothecaries
30	Masons	59	Shipwrights

60 Spectaclemakers
61 Clockmakers
62 Glovers
63 Feltmakers
64 Framework
   Knitters
65 Needlemakers
66 Gardeners
67 Tin Plate
   Workers
68 Wheelwrights
69 Distillers
70 Patternmakers
71 Glass Sellers
72 Coachmakers
73 Gunmakers
74 Gold and Silver
   Wyre Drawers
75 Makers of
   Playing Cards
76 Fanmakers
77 Carmen
*78 Master Mariners
79 Solicitors
80 Farmers
81 Air Pilots and
   Navigators
82 Tobacco Pipe
   Makers

83 Furniture
   Makers
*84 Scientific
   Instrument
   Makers (*hall
   shared with 53*)
85 Chartered
   Surveyors
86 Chartered
   Accountants
87 Chartered
   Secretaries
88 Builders'
   Merchants
89 Launderers
90 Marketors
91 Actuaries
92 Insurers
93 Arbitrators

*Companies without
livery*

Builders
Lightmongers
Master Cleaners
Parish Clerks
Watermen and
Lightermen

OFFICERS OF THE COLLEGE OF ARMS

Granted its first Royal Charter in 1484, the College of Arms (Queen Victoria Street, EC4) deals principally with state ceremonies, the granting of arms and tracing genealogies. The head of the College, known as the Earl Marshal, is a hereditary title held by the Duke of Norfolk. The officers are:

Kings of Arms
Garter King of Arms
Clarenceux King of Arms
Norray and Ulster King of Arms

Heralds
York Herald
Richmond Herald
Windsor Herald
Somerset Herald
Lancaster Herald
Chester Herald

Pursuivants
Portcullis Pursuivant
Rouge Dragon Pursuivant
Rouge Croix Pursuivant
Blue Mantle Pursuivant

TEN LONDON SUPERSTITIONS

The Cuming Museum (155–157 Walworth Road, SE17), based on the collection started by Richard Cuming in 1782, contains the Lovett Collection – a special display of objects relating to London superstitions. Among them are:

1 Horse-brasses representing the sun and moon, worn on the martingales of London cart-horses since Roman times as symbols of the sun and moon gods.

2 A necklace made of stems of woody nightshade, once put round the necks of infants to facilitate teething.

3 A horseshoe covered with red cloth hung over the bed-head to charm away nightmares.

4 A cat skin worn as a cure for rheumatism and chest complaints, introduced from Belgium during the First World War.

5   A cure for whooping cough: hair cut from the back of a child's head is made into a sandwich and given to the first passing dog, who then receives the disease. It was claimed to be effective as recently as 1915.

6   The head of a 14th-century magician's staff, discovered in the Thames, engraved with the Star of David or Solomon's Seal, believed to be a powerful charm against demons.

7   A rare reversed (i.e.: left-handed) whelk shell, carried to ward off danger.

8   Blind-cords in the form of acorns – protections against being struck by lightning.

9   A mandrake root – actually black briony, as mandrake is very rare in England – which reputedly screams when it is uprooted, and was regarded as a cure-all.

10 A pin-cushion carried by sailors as a charm against drowning, acquired in the London Docks in 1917.

TEN LONDON THEME PUBS

Many London pubs have associations with the worlds of literature and the press, law, entertainment and so on, and have built up collections of pictures and other items on a variety of themes. Among the most interesting are:

1   Clanger, 104 Houndsditch, EC3
Great Fire of London and firefighting theme, including fire insurance companies' firemarks – plaques once sited on walls to authenticate insurance cover.

2   Eagle, 2 Shepherdess Walk, N1
Music hall pictures – the pub was once a music hall and features in the song, 'Pop Goes The Weasel'.

3 Edgar Wallace, 40 Essex Street, WC2
Formerly the Essex Head, it was renamed in 1975 on the centenary of the birth of thriller writer Edgar Wallace and contains Wallace memorabilia.

4 Gilbert and Sullivan, 23 Wellington Street, WC2
Operetta mementoes.

5 Giles, 13 Prebend Street, N1
Cartoons by Giles of the *Daily Express*.

6 Grenadier, 18 Wilton Row, SW1
Military paraphernalia – including a sentry box outside.

7 Queen's Elm, 241 Fulham Road, SW3
Antique pipe collection.

8 Railway Tavern, 15 Liverpool Street, EC2
Railway pictures and ephemera.

9 Sherlock Holmes, 10 Northumberland Street, WC2
Sherlock Holmes mementoes and a faithful reconstruction of his Baker Street study, originally exhibited in the 1951 Festival of Britain.

10 Witness Box, 36 Tudor Street, EC4
Crime story newspaper cuttings.

SOME LONDON PUBS WITH STRANGE NAMES

Barmy Arms, The Embankment, Twickenham
Bishop's Finger, 9/10 West Smithfield, EC1
Early John, 54 Holloway Road, N7
Five Bells and Bladebone, 27 Three Colt Street, E14
Frog and Firkin, 41 Tavistock Crescent, W11
Frog and Nightgown, 148 Old Kent Road, SE1
I am the Only Running Footman, 5 Charles Street, W1

Intrepid Fox, 99 Wardour Street, W1
Monkey Puzzle, 30 Southwick Street, W2
Overthrown Cart, Claverings Industrial Estate, N9
Queen's Head and Artichoke, 30 Albany Street, NW1
Tim Bobbin, 1 Lillieshall Road, SW4
The World Turned Upside Down, 145 Old Kent Road, SE1
Ye Old Crutched Friars, 15A Crosswall, EC3

TEN HAUNTED LONDON PUBS

1   The Asylum Tavern, 40 Asylum Road, SE15
The phantom of an old lady dressed in grey with her hair in a
bun haunts this Peckham pub – the only one of this name in
England. In 1982 Teacher's Whiskey sponsored an investiga-
tion to find the twelve most authentically haunted inns in
Britain, and The Asylum Tavern was one of these.

2   The Crown and Horseshoes, Horseshoe Lane, Enfield
Curious happenings at The Crown and Horseshoes in Enfield
are attributed by some to the fact that two separate murders
occurred on the premises in the early part of the last century.
The phenomena include doors being slammed by invisible
hands, inexplicable temperature drops and the appearance of
an apparition described as 'a little old lady'.

3   The Duke of Northumberland, Isleworth
Stories of the haunting of The Duke of Northumberland in
Isleworth appeared in the press in 1979. The ex-CID landlord
told of disembodied footsteps and a poltergeist which swept
glasses from a bar shelf and sent a bucket flying over his wife's
head.

4   The Grenadier, 18 Wilton Row, SW1
London's most famous haunted pub is the 300-year-old Grenadier, close to Hyde Park Corner. Once the Duke of Wellington
and his officers used it as a mess and it was George IV's
favourite local – which caused an outburst of public criticism.
According to legend, a young officer was caught cheating at

cards and his brother officers punished him with a flogging. This was so severe that he died in the cellar. Since then various landlords have experienced psychic disturbances on the anniversary of his death and customers have reported seeing a shadowy figure in an old-fashioned uniform.

5   The King's Arms, 132 Peckham Rye, SE15

One of the most modern of London pubs to be haunted, The King's Arms was rebuilt after being bombed in the Second World War. A number of customers were killed sheltering in the cellar, and the haunting goes back to that tragedy. A barman was quoted in the press as saying, 'I was down in the cellars one night when I heard voices singing along to a piano . . . I was scared out of my wits.' Neighbours of the pub corroborated his story and said that a favourite with the unseen singers is *Lili Marlene*.

6   The King's Cellars, 48 Park Street, Croydon

The King's Cellars in Croydon has an extraordinary reputation for poltergeist activity which has included glasses flying through the air as though carried by invisible hands, wild changes in temperature and all the pub's cash tills jamming at precisely the same moment. The tension created by the haunting has had a destructive effect on the marriages of many couples who have worked there. A full account of this case appears in Colin Wilson's book, *Poltergeist*.

7   The Plough Inn, 196 Clapham High Street, SW4

The top storey of The Plough Inn is haunted by a resident phantom known as Sarah. A barman gave in his notice after seeing a dark-haired woman clothed in white who melted away before his gaze. Members of the staff have described a curious effect the ghost had upon them – a tingling sensation like a mild electric shock which lasted up to a minute.

8   The Spaniards Inn, Hampstead Lane, NW3

Several inns are reputed to be revisited by the ghost of Dick Turpin, but The Spaniards Inn has the best reputation as a haunt for highwaymen. Turpin frequently used its cellars as a hiding-place, and after his execution the familiar sound of his horse, Black Bess, galloping over the Heath to the pub has been heard by a succession of landlords. Today the Inn displays several Turpin mementoes.

9   The Thomas à Becket, 320 Old Kent Road, SE1

The poltergeist activity in this pub was so dramatic that the landlord refused to sleep on the premises. One tradition is that there was an upstairs room with an atmosphere so eerie that customers who wagered that they could stay in it alone for half an hour invariably lost their bets.

10   Ye Olde Gatehouse, Highgate West Hill, N6

One of London's most prominent spectres is Mother Marnes, a sinister figure dressed in black who glides along a gallery in this Highgate pub. According to one legend, a landlord had to be rushed to hospital after glimpsing her. An odd aspect of the haunting is that the ghost never appears when there are children on the premises.

[List specially prepared for *The Londoner's Almanac* by Marc Alexander, author of many books on British folklore and psychic phenomena, including *Haunted Pubs in Britain and Ireland* (Sphere, 1984).]

CABMEN'S SHELTERS

You might have wondered what those large green wooden sheds are doing parked in the road around London. The first ones appeared in 1875 when The Cabmen's Shelter Fund was established 'for the purpose of supplying Cabmen, when on the ranks, with a place of shelter where they can obtain good and wholesome refreshment at very moderate prices' – or, in plainer language, to prevent cab-drivers from hitting the bottle, since a drunk in charge of a Hansom cab was once a pretty terrifying spectacle. At their peak, there were 63 shelters; now there are just 13 of them, the oldest dating from the 1890s:

Chelsea Embankment,
  SW3
Grosvenor Gardens, SW1
Hanover Square, W1
Kensington Park Road,
  W11
Kensington Road, SW7
Leicester Square, WC2

Northumberland Avenue,
  WC2
Pont Street, SW1
St George's Square, SW1
Temple Place, WC2
Thurloe Place, SW7
Warwick Avenue, W9
Wellington Place, NW8

SOME LONDON TAXI FACTS AND FIGURES

* There is no legislation to limit the number of licensed cabs and cab drivers in London. Both have increased in recent years:

	1981	1982	1983	1984
Licensed cabs in service	12385	12809	13127	12780
Licensed drivers	17825	18086	18205	18421

* Cab drivers can be licensed for 'All London' (Green Badge) or for one or more of six specific suburban areas at least six miles from Charing Cross (Yellow Badge). Suburban drivers can take passengers to any area, but cannot pick up from outside their area.

* All drivers have to pass qualifying exams on 'Knowledge of London'. Most applicants train for the 'Knowledge of London' with one of the independent training schools. They travel around mainly on mopeds, learning the location of principal stations, hotels, theatres, etc and shortest routes. They learn 468 well used routes within six miles of Charing Cross, after which they are examined at 56 day intervals by the Public Carriage Office. The periods between these rigorous examinations are reduced to 28, then 14 days and concluded by a final examination. The average time taken to

pass this is 18 months. Drivers must also pass a special driving test.

* Over 3000 people apply for cab licences every year. Of these only 40% are eventually licensed.

* Cabs are licensed annually. Their numbers are issued in sequence in a series of separate thousands for each month of the year – thus those licensed in March, the third month, all bear plates in the 3000 series; in April, 4000, and so on.

Twenty Slang Words used by London Taxi Drivers

Bilker	Customer who refuses to pay.
Bottle	£2.
Brooming-off	Cabbie on a rank passing an unprofitable hiring to the next in line.
Butter-boy	Novice in the trade, but not a total stranger. Said to have appeared during a taxi strike in 1913.
Carpet	£3 (three feet to the yard – the standard carpet measure – though some authorities suggest that it derives from three months, the length of time taken to make a carpet in a prison workshop).
Connaught Ranger	Rhyming slang for stranger – i.e.: a newcomer in the trade. The Connaught Rangers were the 88th Regiment of Foot, disbanded in 1922.

Droshki	Cab; from the Russian, introduced by refugees.
Face	Well-known character; a 1950s term.
Flyer	Trip to London airport.
Gantville	Many cabbies live in Ilford and Gants Hill. Sometimes known as 'Gantville Cowboys', they have considerable lobbying power.
Hanging up	Loitering outside a hotel with the hire sign off, waiting for a porter to offer a lucrative job, rather than taking jobs in the correct order.
Jacks	£5 (rhyming slang for 'Jack's alive').
Legal	Precise fare only, without a tip.
Monkey	£500.
Mush	Owner-driver.
Pin position	First cab on a rank.
Putting on foul	Overloading a taxi rank.
Rouf	£4 ('four', backwards).
Wrong 'un	Bad job.
Zeiger	Taximeter; also known as a 'Jewish piano'.

Forty Punning London Hairdressers' Names

Although most London hairdressers are called something like 'Maison Roger', 'André' or 'Snippers', many have names that are clever puns on the service they offer. Here are forty of them:

Alias Quiff & Combs	Hazel Nutz
Ali Barber	Head First
Beyond the Fringe	Headlines
Blow-Inn	Headmasters
Buzz-Bees	Headway
Curl Up & Dye	Head Start
Cut Above	Heads We Do
Cut Loose	Heads You Win
Deb 'n' Hair	Heatwave
Do Yer Nut	Lunatic Fringe
Fringe Benefits	Mane Attraction
Hair & Now	New Barnet
Hairazors	New Wave
Hair Today	Shear Pleasure
Hair We Are	Shylocks
Hair We Go	Streaks Ahead
Hairloom	Sun 'n' Hair
Hairport	Swiss Hair
Hairs & Graces	Uppercuts
Hats Off	Wavelength

Ten London Words

1 Billingsgate

The use of 'bad language' in the Billingsgate fish market led to 'Billingsgate' entering the language – to mean any sort of slang – at least as early as the seventeenth century.

2 Bloomsbury Group

London and its 'villages' have given their names to many artistic communities, such as the Camden Town School, Fitzrovia, London Group and St John's Wood Clique. 'Bloomsbury', one of the most famous, referred to a group of artists, writers and intellectuals, such as Virginia Woolf and Duncan Grant, who lived in the area from about 1907 to 1930.

3 Camberwell beauty

Nymphalis antiopa, a type of butterfly, now rare, was first recorded in Camberwell in 1748 – when the area was a popular country resort.

4 Carnaby Street

Along with two other terms associated with fashionable London locations – the Chelsea boot and King's Road – 'Carnaby Street' appeared in the 'swinging sixties' as a synonym for any new trend. In the Kinks' song, A Dedicated Follower of Fashion (1966), devotees are satirized as the 'Carnabytian Army' in their slavish conformity to outrageous styles of dress.

5 Clapham omnibus

'The man on the Clapham omnibus', meaning the ordinary, reasonable person, has long been in use, especially among lawyers. The area also gave its name to the Clapham Sect – a group of evangelical Anglicans who settled around Clapham in the late eighteenth and early nineteenth centuries, and included William Wilberforce, the prominent campaigner for the abolition of slavery.

6 Hackney carriages

Although most dictionaries will tell you otherwise, Hackney carriages probably did *not* originate in Hackney. It seems more likely that the name derives from an old French word, *haquenée*, meaning a horse available for hire.

7 Lambeth Quadrilateral

Not, as might be supposed, a square dance version of the Lambeth Walk, a dance popular in the 1930s, but the agreement reached at the 1888 Lambeth Conference on four basic principles for a United Christian Church.

8 Limehouse
Lloyd George was noted for his fiery speeches in Limehouse in 1909 – and thus the word came into use to describe any inflammatory speech. More recently it has become associated with the Social Democratic Party (SDP), the leader of which, David Owen, lives in this newly fashionable part of London.

9 London Rocket
Sisymbrium irio, a plant so-called, according to the seventeenth-century naturalist John Ray, because it shot up like a rocket, rapidly colonizing waste ground after the Great Fire of London.

10 Sloane Ranger
A now widely used phrase invented by Peter York in an article in *Harpers & Queen* in October 1975, to describe a particular upper-class style, with Sloane Square as its geographical centre.

TEN EPONYMS WITH LONDON ASSOCIATIONS

There are literally thousands of eponyms – words in the language that derive from personal names. The following ten all have close connections with London:

1 Belisha beacon
The flashing pedestrian-crossing lights were introduced by Sir Leslie Hore-Belisha (1893–1957) when he was Minister of Transport in 1934.

2 Bobby
The slang term for a policeman was derived from the name of Sir Robert Peel (1788–1850), who as Home Secretary passed the Metropolitan Police Act in 1829.

3 Bowler hat

James Lock and Co., the hatmakers – still in business at 6 St James's Street, SW1 – were asked in 1850 to make a low hat that would not get knocked off the head by low branches while out shooting. Their customer was William Coke – and this is what Locks called the hat; but their suppliers were called Bowler, and it was this name, not Coke's, that stuck when the style became popular.

4 Clerihew

This non-scanning verse form was invented by Edmund Clerihew Bentley (1875–1956) when he was a 16-year-old schoolboy at St Paul's School, London, with:

Sir Humphrey Davy
Abominated gravy,
He lived in the odium
Of having discovered sodium.

5 Diddle

From a play, *Raising the Wind*, by James Kenney (1780–1849), first performed in London in 1903; the central character, a petty crook, was called Jeremy Diddler.

6 Hansom cab

The architect Joseph Aloysius Hansom (1802–82) patented the 'Safety Cab' that bore his name in 1834. By 1886 there were 7020 and in 1904 7499 hansoms on the streets of London. They were eventually ousted by motor cabs – although there were still a dozen hansoms operating up to 1927.

7 Nissen hut

The corrugated steel air raid shelters widely used by Londoners during the Blitz were invented by Lieut.-Col. Peter Nissen (1871–1930), a British mining engineer.

8 Rachmanism

Peter Rachman (1920–62), an unscrupulous London landlord, used harassment to drive out tenants whose rent was fixed under the 1957 Rent Act, thereby giving his name to this practice.

9 Tich

Harry Ralph (1868–1928), a London music hall comedian, derived his stage name 'Little Tich' from the celebrated 'Tichborne Case' of 1867 (during which one Arthur Orton posed as R. C. Tichborne in order to claim his inheritance). Subsequently, 'tich' came into use to describe anyone or anything small.

10 Tradescantia

John Tradescant (1608–62), Court Gardener to King Charles II and collector of botanic specimens, gave his name to this American plant. Tradescant's collection of 'curiosities' became the basis of the Ashmolean Museum, Oxford, and he is buried at St Mary-at-Lambeth – now the Tradescant Trust's museum of gardening history.

FOUR QUOTATIONS ABOUT LONDON

'When a man is tired of London he is tired of life; for there is in London all that life can afford.'
> Dr Johnson (20 September 1777) quoted in James Boswell's *Life of Samuel Johnson*, 1791.

'. . . I naturally gravitated to London, that great cesspool into which all the loungers and idlers of the Empire are irresistibly drained.'
> Sir Arthur Conan Doyle, *A Study in Scarlet*, 1887.

'London, thou art the flour of Cities all.'
> William Dunbar, *In Honour of the City of London*, 1501.

'It was a saying of Lord Chatham, that the parks were the lungs of London.'
> William Windham, MP, in a House of Commons speech, 30 June 1808 (Lord Chatham was the Prime Minister, William Pitt [1708–78]).

FOUR LONDON POEMS

Earth has not anything to show more fair:
Dull would he be of soul who could pass by
A sight so touching in its majesty:
This City now doth, like a garment, wear
The beauty of the morning; silent, bare,
Ships, towers, domes, theatres, and temples lie
Open unto the fields, and to the sky;
All bright and glittering in the smokeless air.
Never did sun more beautifully steep
In his first splendour, valley, rock, or hill;
N'er saw I, never felt, a calm so deep!
The river glideth at his own sweet will:
Dear God! the very houses seem asleep;
And all that mighty heart is lying still!

    William Wordsworth, *Composed Upon Westminster Bridge, 3 September 1803*.

[Wordsworth's sonnet was inspired by the sight of London as he crossed the old Westminster Bridge on the Dover coach as dawn broke.]

Mortality behold and fear
What a change of flesh is here!
Think how many royal bones
Sleep within these heaps of stones:
Here they lie, had realms and lands
Who now want strength to stir their hands:
Where from their pulpits seal'd with dust
They preach, 'In greatness is no trust.'
Here's an acre, sown indeed
With the richest, royall'st seed
That the earth did e'er such in,
Since the first man died for sin.

    Francis Beaumont, *Ode on the Tombs in Westminster Abbey*. Beaumont himself was buried in Westminster Abbey in 1616.

Souls of poets dead and gone,
What Elysium have ye known,
Happy field or mossy cavern,
Choicer than the Mermaid Tavern?
   John Keats, *Lines on the Mermaid Tavern*, 1820.

[The Mermaid Tavern, which stood in Bread Street in the
City, was the meeting-place of notable Elizabethan writers and
poets, including Raleigh, Jonson, Marlowe, Shakespeare and
Donne. It was burned down in the Great Fire of London.]

Twenty bridges from Tower to Kew
Wanted to know what the River knew,
For they were young and the Thames was old,
And this is the story that the River told.
   Rudyard Kipling, *The River's Tale*, 1911.

TEN LONDON SONGS

Burlington Bertie
  from Bow
Down at the Old Bull
  and Bush
A Foggy Day in
  London Town
Knocked 'em in the
  Old Kent Road

The Lambeth Walk
Maybe it's Because
  I'm a Londoner
A Nightingale Sang in
  Berkeley Square
The Streets of London
Up the Junction
Waterloo Sunset

FOUR LONDON NURSERY RHYMES

London Bridge is falling down

London Bridge is falling down,
  Falling down, falling down,
London Bridge is falling down,
  My fair lady.

Oranges and lemons

'Oranges and lemons,' say the bells of St Clements.
'Brickbats and tiles,' say the bells of St Giles.
'You owe me five farthings,' say the bells of St Martin's.
'When will you pay me?' say the bells of Old Bailey.
'When I grow rich,' say the bells of Shoreditch.
'When will that be?' say the bells of Stepney.
'I do not know,' says the great bell of Bow.
Here comes a candle to light you to bed,
And here comes a chopper to chop off your head!

Pussy cat, pussy cat

Pussy cat, pussy cat,
Where have you been?
I've been up to London
To look at the Queen.
Pussy cat, pussy cat,
What did you there?
I frightened a little mouse
Under her chair.

Pop goes the weasel!

Up and down the City Road,
  In and out of the Eagle,
That's the way the money goes,
  Pop goes the weasel!

Half a pound of twopenny rice,
  Half a pound of treacle,
Mix it up and make it nice,
  Pop goes the weasel!

FOUR LONDON CHILDHOOD HEROES

1   Mary Poppins
The Banks family's nanny and her magical powers – which

include sliding *up* bannisters and sailing over London's roof-
tops – are the subject of P. L. Travers' *Mary Poppins* books,
the first of which was published in 1934.

2 Paddington Bear

The bear from 'darkest Peru' makes his debut in Michael
Bond's *A Bear Called Paddington* (1958) when he is found by
the Brown family on Paddington Station – hence his name. He
has a label attached to him which reads, 'Please look after this
bear'. His fondness for marmalade, his duffel coat, wellington
boots and sou'wester have made him a familiar and popular
figure in subsequent books and in a television cartoon series.

3 Peter Pan

Peter Pan was created by J. M. Barrie in his play of the same
name, subtitled *The Boy Who Wouldn't Grow Up*, first per-
formed at the Duke of York's Theatre, London, in 1904.
Barrie published it in book form in 1911 as *Peter Pan and
Wendy*. A statue of Peter Pan in Kensington Gardens – once
voted London's most popular statue – was erected in 1912;
Peter Pan also appears on the memorial to its sculptor, Sir
George Frampton, in St Paul's Cathedral.

4 The Wombles

The Wombles first appeared in Elizabeth Beresford's *The
Wombles* (1968). They are furry creatures who live underground on Wimbledon Common and collect items discarded
by humans, putting them to novel uses. Books, popular songs
and a television series have made them a huge success.

LONDON IN MINIATURE: FOUR MODELS OF NOTABLE LONDON BUILDINGS

Architectural models of many London buildings can be seen in
museums such as the Museum of London and the Victoria and
Albert Museum, but there are also miniature versions of
several important buildings in less familiar places, including:

1 The Bank of England
Sir Charles Wheeler's statue of the 'Old Lady of Threadneedle Street' at the Bank of England is shown holding a model of the building on her knee.

2 St Dionis Backchurch
The old Wren church that stood at the junction of Lime Street and Fenchurch Street appears on the font cover of St Dionis, Parson's Green, which was built from the proceeds of its sale when it was demolished in 1878.

3 St Paul's Cathedral
A model of it is held by one of the bronze female statues on Vauxhall Bridge. Representing 'Architecture', it was made by the sculptors, Frederick Pommeroy and Alfred Drury. A massive wooden architectural model of the Cathedral can be seen in St Paul's Crypt.

4 Temple Bar
The memorial unveiled in 1880, ten years after Temple Bar, formerly at the junction of Fleet Street and Strand, was removed, has on it a relief depicting the Bar.

LONDON'S TEN LARGEST THEATRES AND CONCERT HALLS

THEATRE	CAPACITY*	THEATRE	CAPACITY*
1 Royal Albert Hall	c7000	5 Theatre Royal	2216
2 Royal Festival Hall	3111	6 Royal Opera House	2141
3 Coliseum	2358	7 Barbican Hall	2047
4 London Palladium	2298	8 Prince Edward	1577
		9 Victoria Palace	1560
		10 Adelphi	1510

* Seating capacity may fluctuate according to nature of production.

THE TWENTY LONGEST-RUNNING SHOWS IN LONDON

TITLE	PERFORMANCES
The Mousetrap*	13318 [1]
No Sex, Please – We're British*	5647
Black and White Minstrels	4354 [2]
Oh! Calcutta!	3863
Jesus Christ, Superstar	3401
Life with Father	3213
Evita*	2735
Oliver	2618
There's a Girl in My Soup	2547
Pyjama Tops	2498
The Sound of Music	2386
Sleuth	2359
Salad Days	2283
My Fair Lady	2281
Chu Chin Chow	2238
Charley Girl	2202
The Boy Friend	2084

Canterbury Tales	2 082
Boeing Boeing	2 035
Blithe Spirit	1 997

* Still running – number of performances as at 31 December 1984.
[1] Opened 25 November 1952 at Ambassador's Theatre; after 8862 performances transferred to St Martin's Theatre where it re-opened on 25 March 1974.
[2] Continuous performances; with the 1973 revival the total is 6464 performances.

TEN ROCK STARS WHO DIED YOUNG IN LONDON

1 Marc Bolan, 29
Lead singer with T-Rex, killed in a car crash on Barnes Common, 16 September 1977.

2 Graham Bond, 37
Founder of the Graham Bond Organization, died under a tube train at Finsbury Park station, 8 May 1974.

3 John 'Bonzo' Bonham, 31
Drummer with Led Zeppelin, died of asphyxiation at Windsor, 25 September 1980.

4 Sandy Denny, 37
Lead singer of Fairport Convention, died of a cerebral haemorrhage after falling downstairs, 21 April 1978.

5   Cass Elliot, 30
Singer with The Mamas and The Papas, died of a heart attack,
29 July 1974.

6   Pete Farndon, 29
Bass guitarist with The Pretenders, died of a drug overdose, 14
April 1983.

7   Jimi Hendrix, 27
Singer and guitarist, dead on arrival at St Mary Abbots
Hospital after inhaling vomit during barbiturate overdose, 18
September 1970.

8   Paul Kossoff, 25
Guitarist with Free, died on a flight out of London, cause
uncertain, 19 March 1976.

9   Jimmy McCulloch, 25
Guitarist with Wings, found dead in his flat, cause uncertain,
27 September 1979.

10   Keith Moon, 31
Drummer with The Who, died after an overdose of
Hemenephrin, 7 September 1978.

[Taken from *The Day the Music Died: A Rock and Roll Tribute*, various authors, Plexus, 1985.]

TWENTY HOLLYWOOD STARS
WHO WERE BORN IN LONDON

Name	Born
Claire Bloom	1931
Dirk Bogarde	1921
Michael Caine	1933

Charlie Chaplin	1889
Gladys Cooper	1888
Noel Coward	1899
Edward Fox	1937
Stewart Granger	1913
Alfred Hitchcock	1899
Bob Hope	1903
Leslie Howard	1890
Boris Karloff	1887
Elsa Lanchester	1902
Peter Lawford	1923
Roger Moore	1928
Anna Neagle	1904
Oliver Reed	1938
Sir C. Aubrey Smith	1863
Elizabeth Taylor	1932
Peter Ustinov	1921

FILM TITLES FEATURING LONDON DISTRICTS

The Bermondsey Kid (1933)

Les Bicyclettes de Belsize (1968)

The Bloomsbury Burglars (1912)

Britannia of Billingsgate (1933)

Chelsea Life (1933)

Chelsea Nights (1929)

Chelsea Story (1951)

The Duchess of Seven Dials (1920)

Emmanuelle in Soho (1981)

The Lambeth Walk (1939)

Man of Mayfair (1931)

Mayfair Girl (1933)

Mayfair Melody (1937)

Maytime in Mayfair (1949)

A Murder in Limehouse (1919)

Murder in Mayfair (1942)

Murder in Soho (1939)

Passport to Pimlico (1949)

A Romance of Mayfair (1925)

Horace of Putney (1923)
The Kensington Mystery
 (1924)
The King of Seven
 Dials (1914)

Soho Conspiracy (1950)
Soho Incident (1956)
The Soho Murders (1942)
Tilly of Bloomsbury
 (1921)

LONDON STREETS AND SQUARES IN FILM TITLES

The Barretts of Wimpole
 Street (1934 & 1956)
The Black Sheep of
 Whitehall (1941)
Bond Street (1948)
Charing Cross Road
 (1935)
The Courtneys of Curzon
 Street (1947)
East of Ludgate Hill
 (1937)
East of Piccadilly
 (1941)
The Girl from Downing
 Street (1918)
Greek Street (1930)
Hyde Park Corner (1935)
I Live in Grosvenor
 Square (1945)
It Happened in Leicester
 Square (1949)
The Lavender Hill Mob
 (1951)
The Lonely Lady from
 Grosvenor Square
 (1922)

No 5 John Street (1922)
A Park Lane Scandal
 (1915)
Piccadilly (1929)
Piccadilly Incident
 (1946)
Piccadilly Nights
 (1930)
Piccadilly Playtime
 (1936)
Piccadilly Third Stop
 (1960)
The Seer of Bond Street
 (1913)
77 Park Lane (1931)
The Siege of Sidney
 Street (1960)
Spring in Park Lane
 (1948)
10 Rillington Place
 (1970)
Waterloo Road (1945)
A Window in Piccadilly
 (1928)

[This list and the preceding list specially prepared for *The Londoner's Almanac* by Patrick Robertson, author of *The Guinness Book of Film Facts and Feats* (Guinness Superlatives, 1985).]

TEN FAMOUS LONDON ADDRESSES

1 10 Downing Street

Sir George Downing, MP, built the street in about 1680. No. 10 became the official residence of the Prime Minister in 1732, when the eastern part was acquired by the Crown, followed by the western part in 1763. The interior was extensively rebuilt in the eighteenth and nineteenth centuries and in recent times. The nature of the latest changes is an Official Secret.

2 'No. 1 London'

Apsley House at Hyde Park Corner, built in 1771–78, was the London home of the Duke of Wellington. So famous was he that in his lifetime letters addressed to 'No. 1 London' invariably reached him – though its name may derive from the fact that it was once the first large house encountered by travellers entering London from the west. The Wellington Museum now occupies Apsley House.

3 54 Berners Street

In 1809 a practical joker, Theodore Hook, bet a playwright called Sam Beazley one guinea that he could make 54 Berners Street the most famous house in London. The unfortunate victim of the hoax that followed was an old widow called Mrs Tottingham. Using her name, Hook ordered all manner of tradesmen from chimney sweeps and dentists to undertakers and midwives to deliver goods or make collections from the house. Various ruses even allegedly resulted in visits from the Archbishop of Canterbury, the Lord Chief Justice, the Lord Mayor and the Governor of the Bank of England. Before the hoax was exposed, this insignificant house had indeed become – temporarily – the most famous address in London.

4 1A Cato Street

On the evening of 23 February 1820, a room above a stable in Cato Street (formerly No. 6, but now 1A) became the violent scene of the thwarting of the so-called 'Cato Street Conspiracy'. The plotters, led by Arthur Thistlewood, were planning to storm the Grosvenor Square house of Lord Harrowby, where members of the British cabinet were dining. Their murder was to be followed by the capture of notable institutions such as the Bank of England and Tower of London and the installation of a provisional government. But betrayed by one of their number, the conspirators' plan was foiled, and the Cato Street headquarters was raided by police and soldiers. The ringleaders were captured and hanged or transported. A blue plaque commemorates the event.

5 50 Wimpole Street
Now demolished, this was the home of Elizabeth Barrett for the eight years prior to her elopement and secret marriage to Robert Browning in 1846. Their love story has been immortalised by the 1934 film, *The Barretts of Wimpole Street*, and its remake in 1956.

6 221 Baker Street
One of London's most widely known addresses – the home of Sir Arthur Conan Doyle's Sherlock Holmes – never existed. In his day, the highest number in Baker Street was 85. There was no 221 until 1930, but this fictional address became so famous that Abbey National, the building society that occupies 221, continues to receive letters addressed to the great detective.

7 19 Cleveland Street
In 1889, Ernest Parke, the editor of the *North London Press*, conducted 'investigative journalism' of a decidedly modern kind. Two men, a minister called Veck and a young man called Newlove, had been given fairly light sentences after being arrested by the police during a raid on 19 Cleveland Street, which, it was revealed – in the coyest possible language of the day – was a homosexual brothel. Since sentences for similar offences were usually heavy, Parke delved and published a story to the effect that a cover-up had been engineered to protect one of the house's habituees, Lord Euston – if not the Prince of Wales himself. Lord Euston sued Parke for libel. Parke was found guilty and jailed for a year. The full facts of the case have never been revealed.

8   50 Berkeley Square

Once the home of Prime Minister George Canning, the house –
now occupied by Maggs & Co, the antiquarian booksellers – is
said to be haunted by a ghost so hideous that an army officer
who once braved a night in the haunted bedroom shot himself.

9   10 Rillington Place

In 1949, Timothy Evans confessed to and was hanged for
murdering his wife and daughter at this Notting Hill address.
Four years later, the remains of six further women were found
in the house and garden and another resident, John Christie,
was charged with their murder and that of Evans' wife and
child. He was also executed and Evans was eventually granted
(posthumously) a free pardon. The appalling associations of
the street led to its renaming, and it was ultimately demolished.

10   84 Charing Cross Road

The address of the secondhand bookshop, Marks & Co,
acquired fame when it was used as the title of a book by Helene
Hanff. Miss Hanff, an American author, began writing to the
shop in 1949 in search of out-of-print books. Although she
never met him, her correspondence with Frank Doel, a member of staff, developed into a warm transatlantic friend-
ship. Their letters, spanning twenty years, became the basis
of a bestselling book and have been made into a successful
theatrical performance.

BLUE PLAQUE LEAGUE TABLE

Blue plaques showing where famous people lived in London
have been erected since the 1860s. There are now 491 of them.
The decision to erect a plaque is made by the Historic Buildings Board of the GLC, which establishes the authenticity of a
candidate's associations with the building in question. Among

the Board's criteria are that the person should be regarded as eminent, should be 'known to the well-informed passer-by', and have been dead for twenty years – although people can be considered after the centenary of their births, if this is earlier. The GLC does not have responsibility for plaques in the City of London, and there are certain boroughs where no one sufficiently famous is deemed to have lived. The league table is thus:

Borough	No. of plaques	Borough	No. of plaques
Westminster	195	Harrow	3
Kensington and Chelsea	92	Bromley	2
		Hounslow	2
Camden	82	Redbridge	2
Wandsworth	19	Bexley	1
Hammersmith	14	Brent	1
Lambeth	13	Ealing	1
Tower Hamlets	12	Merton	1
Islington	10	Sutton	1
Greenwich	9	Waltham	
Lewisham	7	Forest	1
Richmond	5	Barking	0
Croydon	4	Enfield	0
Hackney	4	Havering	0
Southwark	4	Hillingdon	0
Barnet	3	Kingston	0
Haringey	3	Newham	0

[Figures as at 31 December 1984]

Ten London Street Names and Their Origins

1 Billiter Square, EC3
From the word, 'belyeter' or 'bellzeter', a bellfounder whose factory was once located here to serve the numerous City churches.

2 Bunhill Row, EC1
Named after nearby Bunhill Fields, which derives its name from the 'Bone Hill', a macabre heap of human bones dumped here when St Paul's Cathedral's charnel house was cleared in 1549.

3 Camomile Street, EC2
Named after the medicinal plant that once grew there – nearby Wormwood Street further emphasises that London's most built-up area was once extensively cultivated.

4 Fetter Lane, EC4
There are several explanations for the origin of the name:
faitour – an idler or vagabond;
fewter – a rest for a spear, or *fetter* – a shackle, both from the connection with the Knights Templars' armourers who had workshops in the area;
fetor – an offensive smell (though since most of London once stank, it is not clear why this area should have been singled out);
frater – brother, from the many lawyers who worked nearby.

5 King's Road, SW3/6/10
This was once, quite literally, the King's private road, used by Charles II on journeys between St James's Palace and Hampton Court. Others could obtain a special pass, but it did not become a public thoroughfare until 1830.

6 Leadenhall Street, EC3
Named after the market which stood outside the mansion belonging to the Neville family, built for Sir Hugh Neville in

about 1320. It had a lead roof and was thus known as the 'leaden hall'.

7 Mount Street, W1
This unlikely name for a street in a notably flat part of the West End comes from 'Oliver's Mount', an earthwork said to have been erected in 1643 when London was fortified during the Civil War.

8 Pall Mall, SW1
The game of pall mall, a kind of croquet played with a wooden mallet and balls, was popular in the sixteenth century when it was introduced from Italy (it derives from *palla*, a ball, and *maglio*, a mallet) but became particularly fashionable under Charles II who had a pall mall alley constructed in St James's Field – later St James's Park. The street now known as Pall Mall runs close to the north side of the park. Although originally known as Catharine Street, it came to be called after the game.

9 Strand, WC2
Before the building of the Embankment, the street known as the Strand was actually on the bank, or strand, of the Thames. Progressive building encroachments over the centuries have pushed the bank back by several hundred feet.

10 Temeraire Street, SE16
Named after the warship *Temeraire*, which had fought at the battle of Trafalgar in 1805 and was broken up at the yard of Beatson, a local firm, in 1838. The destruction of this once noble vessel attracted much public attention: it was the subject of a song and of J. M. W. Turner's famous painting, *The 'Fighting Temeraire' Tugged to Her Last Berth To Be Broken Up*, 1838, now in the National Gallery.

AN A–Z OF LONDON'S STRANGEST STREET NAMES

Asylum Road, SE15
Boss Street, SE1
Crooked Usage, N3
Dog Kennel Hill, SE22
Effort Street, SW17
Frying Pan Alley, E1
Gutter Lane, EC2
Ha Ha Road, SE18
Idol Lane, EC3
Jews Row, SW18
Kitcat Terrace, E3
Lizard Street, EC1
Mount Nod Road, SW16
Nuding Close, SE13

Ogle Street, W1
Pickle Herring Street, SE1
Quex Road, NW6
Rabbit Row, W8
Straightsmouth, SE10
Tweezer's Alley, WC2
Uamvar Street, E14
Voluntary Place, E11
Weltje Road, W6
XX Place, E1 (recently demolished)
Yeo Street, E3
Zampa Road, SE16

EIGHT NOTABLE LONDON COURTESANS

1 Madam Cresswell c1625–84

One of the most successful prostitutes of her day, she gained a great deal of influence, wealth and a reputation for outspoken behaviour. She left £10 for the poor on condition that a clergyman spoke well of her, so he said: 'She was born well, she lived well and she died well; for she was born with the name of Cresswell, she lived in Clerkenwell and Camberwell, and she died in Bridewell.'

2 Barbara Villiers 1641–1709

The Countess of Castlemaine and Duchess of Cleveland, Barbara Villiers was highly influential at Court and a notorious courtesan. Among her lovers were Jacob Hall, a rope dancer whom she discovered at Bartholomew Fair, and John Churchill, Duke of Marlborough, but she spent about fourteen years as mistress to Charles II, bearing him five children.

3 Nell Gwyn c1650–87
Nell Gwyn began her career as an orange seller at the Theatre Royal, Drury Lane. She became the mistress of the actor, Charles Hart, and took up acting. Hart was followed briefly by Lord Buckhurst, but Nell became one of Charles II's favourites. He set her up in a house on Pall Mall and they remained close until his death.

4 Laura Bell 1829–94
Born in Ireland, the daughter of a bailiff on Lord Hertford's estates, she achieved success as a prostitute in Belfast before moving to London where she set up shop in Wilton Crescent, becoming known as the 'Queen of London whoredom'. In later life she became, rather surprisingly, an evangelical preacher. She married Augustus Thistlethwayte, whose life mysteriously ended in 1887 when he accidentally shot himself.

5 Catherine Walters 1839–1920
Commemorated by an unofficial blue plaque on her house at 15 South Street, W1, as 'the last Victorian courtesan', she was known as 'Skittles' from an incident when she told a group of guardsmen that she would knock them down like 'a row of bloody skittles'. An accomplished horsewoman, she attracted huge crowds whenever she appeared in Hyde Park – even prompting a letter of complaint to *The Times* that she was distracting visitors to the 1862 International Exhibition. Among her friends she could number the Prince of Wales and Lord Kitchener as well as Gladstone – who attempted to reform her.

6 Cora Pearl 1842–86
Born Emma Elizabeth Crouch in Plymouth, she moved to London where she worked as a milliner in Regent Street. There she began a turbulent career as a courtesan which she pursued to Paris. She had numerous lovers and among her many well-documented exploits it was recorded that she was once served naked at a dinner party.

7 Lillie Langtry 1853–1929

The daughter of the Dean of Jersey, she moved to London with her husband, Edward Langtry, and was hailed as a great beauty, nicknamed 'Jersey Lillie'. She became the mistress of the Prince of Wales, Crown Prince Rudolf of Austria and King Leopold of Belgium among many others. Apart from accepting generous gifts from her wealthy patrons, she pursued a successful career as an actress and retired to Monaco in 1919.

8 Frances Warwick 1861–1938

Known as 'Daisy', she married Charles Greville, Lord Brooke, the heir to the 4th Earl of Warwick, in 1881, but had many aristocratic lovers, among them the Prince of Wales between 1891–1900. Under the influence of W. J. Stead and Robert Blatchford of *The Clarion* she turned from socialite to socialist, standing as a Labour candidate in the parliamentary elections of 1923.

MARK BOXER'S TEN BEST PLACES FOR A RENDEZVOUS

1 The Royal Botanic Gardens, Kew

The Temperate House, or anywhere at Kew – the best 15 pence worth in London (or rather, Surrey).

2 The Palm Court at the Ritz

Everything a Palm Court should be – Edwardian, pinkish and with a charming head waiter. A fine place for an assignation over a cocktail.

3 Sir John Soane's Museum, Lincoln's Inn Fields

Meet on the first floor of this small, quiet and mysterious house.

4 Jermyn Street

If you like cheese, arrange to meet at Paxton & Whitfield's; at Floris if you like scent.

5   In a bookshop

If you like a crush, try John Sandoe's in Blacklands Terrace, near Peter Jones, or, if you're in Bloomsbury, Dillons. Waterstone's in Old Brompton Road and the Pan Bookshop in Fulham Road are both open until 10.30 p.m. on weekdays.

6   The Pavilion in the middle of Berkeley Square

At night you have to climb the railings.

7   Art galleries and museums

Opposite the Cranachs at the National Gallery, or the Rex Whistler mural in the Tate Gallery restaurant, where the food is pretty good too. In wet weather, the British Museum has not lost its charm.

8   The King's Head and Eight Bells, Cheyne Walk

If the weather is fine, meet in the minute garden outside this sixteenth-century pub. The lights of the Albert Bridge wink cheerily in the middle distance.

9   Berry Bros & Rudd, St James's

This wine merchant retains its eighteenth-century ambiance, with a sloping floor and human weighing machine. You will have to order a case, but for such a grand firm their prices are very reasonable for good stuff – except their ordinary red wine.

10   Claridge's

Give the Causserie and the orchestra a wide berth and make straight for one of the top floor ex-maids' bedrooms or any bathroom.

[List specially prepared for *The Londoner's Almanac* by Mark Boxer, Editor of *Tatler* and cartoonist ('Marc').]

WILLIAM HICKEY'S TEN BEST PLACES TO GET YOURSELF GOSSIPED ABOUT

Women

1 At the window corner table of Langan's Brasserie (millionairess Olga Deterding was reputed to sit there naked).
2 In the House of Commons tearoom with Jonathan Aitken (he's *so* choosy).
3 In the Officers' Night-room at Buck House (be the first to know who Andy and Eddy bring home while Mum's at Windsor).
4 On gossip column photographer Richard Young's roll of film ('Shall I tell my husband, or just hope the *Express* doesn't print it?')
5 At Nigel Dempster's barbers (they'll all want to know . . .).

Men

1 On the dance floor at Annabel's, with the lady herself.
2 At the Hippodrome on a Monday night (unless you're already gay).
3 In Bubbles Rothermere's boudoir (you can learn how many sorts of champagne she serves).
4 In the seventh-floor gents at the Stock Exchange (join Britain's *jeunesse dorée* giving itself a nosebleed).
5 On Joan Collins' arm at London airport.

[List specially prepared for *The Londoner's Almanac* by Christopher Wilson, 'William Hickey' of the *Daily Express*.]

NINE RECIPES PIONEERED IN LONDON

1 London Buns
These long, icing-sugar-covered buns have been made in London for so long that their origin has been forgotten.

2 Maids of Honour
These rich cakes containing such ingredients as almonds, butter, rennet, brandy and cinnamon inside puff pastry are said to have been named after the maids of honour who attended Queen Elizabeth I at Richmond Palace.

3 Sandwiches
John Montagu, 4th Earl of Sandwich, is alleged to have had his servant put roast beef between slices of bread so that he could continue a marathon card game uninterrupted. Similar methods of eating were known at least as early as Roman times, but his name became irrevocably linked with this most familiar of foods – though his family attempted to rehabilitate his memory by insisting he invented 'sandwiches' because he was so busy with affairs of state.

4 Chelsea Buns
These fruit-filled buns were baked at the once famous Chelsea Bun House which stood at the corner of Pimlico Road and Lower Sloane Street and was patronized by royalty and other visitors to nearby Ranelagh Gardens in the 18th century. It was demolished in 1839.

5 Tom Collins
This gin-based drink is said to have been named after a nineteenth-century barman at Limmer's Old House.

6 Salisbury Steak
Nothing to do with the town of Salisbury, this 'hamburger-without-the-bun' derives from the healthy eating plan formulated by the eminent nineteenth-century physician and nutri-

tionist, Dr James Salisbury. The patriotic attempt to introduce the name to oust the Germanic 'hamburger' during the two World Wars was largely unsuccessful.

7 Pêche Melba
Invented by Auguste Escoffier, the chef at the Savoy, as a tribute to Dame Nellie Melba, the famous Australian opera singer. A modified version was later 'unveiled' at the opening of the Carlton Hotel on 15 July 1899. 'Melba Toast' was also said to have been pioneered at the Savoy.

8 Omelette Arnold Bennett
This haddock-and-cream-filled omelette is another dish originated by the Savoy. It was created for the writer (whose novel, *Imperial Palace*, is set in the hotel) as a quickly-prepared meal when he dined there after attending the theatre as a drama critic.

9 Buck's Fizz
The mixture of champagne and orange juice known as 'Buck's Fizz' is said to have been invented by a barman at Buck's Club, Clifford Street, in the 1920s.

FIVE UNUSUAL LONDON DINNERS

1 On the top of St Paul's Cathedral
In 1820, a new cross and ball were mounted on the dome of St Paul's, to the design of the Cathedral Surveyor, Charles Robert Cockerell. To celebrate its installation, a lunch was held inside it.

2 At the top of Nelson's Column
On 23 October 1843 14 people ate a draughty dinner on the platform surmounting Nelson's Column, just before the statue was erected.

3 Inside a prehistoric monster

On New Year's Eve, 1853, Professor Richard Owen – later head of the Natural History department of the British Museum – chaired a dinner inside the framework of a model of a gigantic iguanodon at Crystal Palace. One of several brick and iron models, they were built by Waterhouse Hawkins under Owen's supervision, and can still be seen in Crystal Palace Park.

4 In a gondola at the Savoy Hotel

In 1905 American businessman George A. Kessler celebrated his birthday by having the courtyard of the Savoy flooded and decorated with backgrounds depicting Venetian scenes. His two dozen dinner guests sat in a huge gondola decorated with 12 000 carnations. The entertainment was provided by Caruso and an elephant made an appearance with a five-foot birthday cake on its back. Unfortunately, a number of swans also scheduled to appear were poisoned by the blue dye in the water.

5 Inside the 'Quadriga'

The massive sculpture of a chariot, or quadriga, drawn by four horses which surmounts Constitution Arch at Hyde Park Corner, was the setting for a dinner for eight given by its sculptor, Adrian Jones, just before its unveiling in 1912.

SHOPPING LIST FOR LONDON'S GREATEST BLOW-OUT

A manuscript said to have been found in the Tower of London lists the ingredients for a banquet to end all banquets, organized by the Earl of Warwick to commemorate the installation of the Duke of York in 1470. It was prepared by 62 cooks backed up by 515 kitchen helpers, and served by 1000 waiters.

300 Quarters of wheat
[1 quarter =
8 bushels]
300 Tuns of Ale
[1 tun = 2 pipes
or 210 gallons]
104 Tuns of Wine
1 Pipe of Spiced Wine
[1 pipe =
105 gallons]
10 Fat Oxen
6 Wild Bulls
300 Pigs
1004 Wethers [rams]
300 Hogs
3000 Calves
300 Capons
100 Peacocks
200 Cranes
200 Kids
2000 Chickens
4000 Pigeons
4000 Rabbits
4000 Ducks
204 Bitterns
400 Hernsies [herons]

200 Pheasants
500 Partridges
5000 Woodcocks
400 Plovers
100 Curlews
100 Quails
1000 Eggets [possibly
egrets, a kind of
heron]
200 Rees [a kind of
sandpiper]
4000 Bucks, Does and
Roebucks
155 Hot Venison
Pasties
4000 Cold Venison
Pasties
1000 Dishes of
Jellies
2000 Hot Custards
4000 Cold Custards
400 Tarts
300 Pikes
300 Breams
8 Seals
4 Porpoises

[Quoted in Alexis Soyer, *The Pantropheon, or History of Food*, London, 1853.]

THE COST OF LIVING IN LONDON

The United Nations produces a table of statistics showing the relative cost of living of its officials around the world. Clearly UN officials' expenditure is far from typical, but the result throws an interesting light on the position of London in the international league table. The index is based on New York = 100.

Conkary, Guinea	157
Damascus, Syria	141
Tokyo, Japan	137
Luanda, Angola	129
Muscat, Oman	120
Cairo, Egypt	107
Tripoli, Libya	114
Copenhagen, Denmark	96
Port au Prince, Haiti	95
London	**95**
Vienna, Austria	95
Washington DC	94
Paris	90
Bogotá, Colombia	90
La Paz, Bolivia	83
Kuala Lumpur, Malaysia	77
Valetta, Malta	61
Budapest, Hungary	51
Managua, Nicaragua	36

LONDON'S TEN MOST EXPENSIVE HOTEL SUITES

Hotel	£ per night	Hotel	£ per night
Intercontinental	590	Claridges	350
Dorchester	550	Connaught	345
Hilton	470	Savoy	320
Ritz	405	Berkeley	320
Hyde Park	400	Grosvenor House	260

TOURIST EXPENDITURE IN LONDON BY COUNTRY OF ORIGIN

Country	£ millions	%
USA	519	25.8
Middle East	320	15.8
West Germany	84	4.2
Australia	71	3.5
France	68	3.4
Italy	61	3.0
Canada	60	3.0
Switzerland	52	2.6
Netherlands	45	2.3
Spain	39	1.9
South Africa	38	1.9
Sweden	38	1.9
Latin America	33	1.7
Greece	32	1.6
Norway	31	1.6
Japan	28	1.4
Belgium and Luxembourg	23	1.1
Denmark	22	1.1
Other countries	449	22.2
TOTAL	2013	100.0

LONDONERS' COUNTRIES OF BIRTH*

UNITED KINGDOM

England	5 175 979
Wales	79 009
Scotland	109 901
Northern Ireland	36 322

UK (part not stated)	855
Channel Islands	2 733
Isle of Man	777
United Kingdom total:	5 405 576

OUTSIDE UNITED KINGDOM
| Irish Republic | 199 253 |
| Ireland (part not stated) | 207 |

Old Commonwealth
Australia	16 409
Canada	10 082
New Zealand	10 573

New Commonwealth
AFRICA
EAST AFRICA
Kenya	50 646
Malawi	2 709
Tanzania	13 949
Uganda	21 632
Zambia	2 660

SOUTH AFRICA
| Botswana, Lesotho and Swaziland | 257 |
| Zimbabwe | 4 241 |

WEST AFRICA
Gambia	271
Ghana	11 995
Nigeria	19 296
Sierra Leone	2 434

CARIBBEAN
Barbados	15 350
Jamaica	86 094
Trinidad and Tobago	9 710
West Indies Associated States	7 670
West Indies (so stated)	5 776
Other Caribbean Commonwealth	26 550
Belize	218
Guyana	16 031

ASIA
SOUTH ASIA

Bangladesh	22 102
India	139 140
Sri Lanka	14 024

FAR EAST

Hong Kong	14 536
Malaysia	16 468
Singapore	6 737

MEDITERRANEAN

Cyprus	58 453
Gibraltar	2 875
Malta and Gozo	7 637

REMAINDER OF THE NEW COMMONWEALTH

Mauritius	12 878
Seychelles	1 104
Other New Commonwealth	1 800

Foreign

Africa

Algeria	830
Egypt	9 606
Libya	1 409
Morocco	3 833
Tunisia	1 263
Republic of South Africa	15 645
Other Africa	6 942

America

USA	22 003
Caribbean	1 028
Central America	1 070
South America	10 478

Asia

Pakistan	35 616
Burma	4 704

People's Republic of China	4 965
Japan	7 964
Philippines	8 264
Vietnam	1 939
Other Asia	5 437

Middle East

Iran	12 396
Israel	4 238
Other Middle East	13 451

Europe

EEC

Belgium	3 747
Denmark	2 452
France	13 978
Italy	30 752
Luxembourg	122
Netherlands	4 643
Federal Republic of Germany	13 232
Germany (part not stated)	16 303
Greece	6 083

REMAINDER OF EUROPE

Albania	50
Austria	8 241
Bulgaria	390
Czechoslovakia	4 085
Finland	1 646
German Democratic Republic	960
Hungary	5 274
Norway	1 425
Poland	25 780
Portugal	10 872
Romania	1 312
Spain	20 982
Sweden	2 301
Switzerland	4 203
Yugoslavia	3 498
Other Europe	247

Turkey	7955
USSR	7250
Rest of the world, and at sea/in the air	381
Outside United Kingdom total:	1203012
TOTAL	**6608588**

* In Greater London at the time of the 1981 Census

THE POPULATION OF LONDON

Accurate assessments of the population have been possible only since the introduction of censuses in 1801. Figures for earlier periods are therefore estimates. There has been a general trend towards depopulation since the 1930s – the Greater London peak of 1939 estimated as 8615050 has now fallen by almost 2 million, and the population of inner London is almost 1 million less than it was a century ago.

60AD	30000
3rd cent.	45–50000
Late 11th cent.	14–18000
1340	40–50000
1600	200000
1700	600000
1750	650000

	County of London only	Greater London total
1801	959310	1096784
1851	2363341	2651939
1901	4536267	6506889
1951	3347982	8193921
1983	2508600	6754500

LONDON'S TOP TEN – THE CAPITAL'S TALLEST BUILDINGS

Building	Height in feet
National Westminster Tower, Old Broad Street, EC2	600
London Telecom Tower (Formerly the Post Office Tower), Howland Street, W1	580
Shakespeare Tower, Barbican, EC2	419
Euston Centre, Euston Road, NW1	408
London Hilton Hotel, 22 Park Lane, W1	405
Centrepoint, 101 New Oxford Street, WC1	398
Britannic House, Moor Lane, EC2	395
Commercial Union, Leadenhall Street, EC3	387
Millbank Tower, Millbank, SW1	387
London Forum Hotel, Cromwell Road, SW7	380

[All ten are modern constructions, but by extending the list by just one, St Paul's Cathedral at 366 feet would rank as London's eleventh tallest building.]

LONDON BENEATH THE PAVEMENT: TEN SUBTERRANEAN SITES

1 Sources of the Fleet river
The Whitestone Pond on Hampstead Heath is not, as is popularly believed, the source of the Fleet – it is an artificial pond created by the Metropolitan Drinking Fountain and Cattle Trough Association. The Fleet actually arises in Hampstead and Highgate ponds and flows under Haverstock and Highgate Hills, uniting under Hawley Road, north of Camden Town station, proceeding down Pancras Way to King's Cross, through Holborn and under Farringdon Road, joining the Thames at Blackfriars Bridge. It functions as a sewer along much of its length. [See also *Ten London Rivers and Canals*, p. 48.]

2   The crypt of St Paul Covent Garden

Covent Garden, WC2

Designed by Inigo Jones as 'the handsomest barn in Europe', and rebuilt in 1798 by Thomas Hardwick after it had been extensively damaged by fire. Most of the gravestones were removed while the churchyard was being levelled, but the vaults of the church probably house the remains of more famous people than any other London church after Westminster Abbey and St Paul's Cathedral, including Samuel Butler (d.1680), author of *Hudibras*, Dr Thomas Arne (d.1778), composer of 'Rule Britannia', Thomas Rowlandson (d.1827), the watercolour painter and Grinling Gibbons (d.1721), the woodcarver.

3   Sir John Soane's Museum basement and crypt

13 Lincoln's Inn Fields, WC2

Built by the architect, Sir John Soane (1753–1837), the 'Monk's Parlour' is part of the monastic suite he installed in his house, now a museum. A corridor opens to the catacombs which were originally lined with tiers of recesses containing cinerary urns. In the sepulchral chamber stands the sarcophagus of the Egyptian pharaoh, Seti I.

4   Brompton Cemetery

Old Brompton Road, SW10

Originally called the West of London and Westminster Cemetery, it was opened in 1840 as one of the first cemeteries built to cope with the overcrowding of London's churchyards. The classical chapel and mausolea were designed by Benjamin Baud, but financial difficulties meant he was unable to complete the proposed network of catacombs. Among notable people buried here were Sir Henry Cole (d.1882), principal organizer of the Great Exhibition of 1851, and the leading Suffragette, Emmeline Pankhurst (d.1928).

5   Baker Street underground station

Marylebone Road and Baker Street, NW1

One of the stations of the Metropolitan Railway from Paddington to Farringdon Street, built during 1862–63, it was opened on 10 January 1863. It was the first underground railway in the world, becoming part of the former 'Inner Circle', completed in 1884. It was constructed by the 'cut and cover' technique, not by tunnelling. The platforms were first partly lit by natural daylight through a series of shafts. The 1863 platforms have been recently restored to something of their original Victorian style, with replicas of the original seats.

6 Abbey Mills Pumping Station
Abbey Lane, E15
Designed by Joseph Bazalgette and opened in 1869 as part of the system of high-, mid- and low-level interceptor sewers catering for the metropolis, the pumping station dealt with the flow from the lowest of the principal sewers. The original station was equipped with eight beam engines driving pumps with a total capacity of 508 cubic metres a minute. These were replaced in 1931–33 by eight electrically driven centrifugal pumps, but the beam engines are still on view.

7 Holborn–Kingsway underpass
Holborn, WC2
Excavated as Kingsway (opened 1905) was built above, it was originally the Kingsway Tram Tunnel. It was enlarged in 1931 to take double-decker buses and was the nexus of the tramway system until 1952. Later it was converted into a road underpass, carrying northbound traffic from Waterloo Bridge to Kingsway.

8 The Post Office railway
Although there were earlier attempts to build railways for the transport of mail underground, the one opened in 1927 between Paddington and Whitechapel was the first practical one. Over six miles in length, it links six sorting offices, including the principal one at Mount Pleasant, carrying about 50 000 mailbags a day at a speed of 35 mph. The electric trains are 27 ft long, with four containers capable of holding fifteen bags of letters or six of parcels in each.

9 County Hall basement and sub-basement
County Hall, SE1
The vast complex beneath County Hall, the headquarters of

the Greater London Council, contains the services that underpin the country's largest local authority. The basement and sub-basement are .98 miles in length and house the gas, water, sewage and electricity services that keep the offices and approximately six miles of corridor above functioning. The pipes are all colour coded: waste and sewage are green; compressed air, light blue; steam, silver grey; drainpipes, black; town gas, yellow ochre; oil, brown; fire safety, red; chemicals, violet.

10   Cabinet War Rooms
King Charles Square, SW1
Recently opened to the public, these underground emergency headquarters were used by Winston Churchill's wartime government. They consist of 6 acres of blast-proof rooms, 40 feet below street level.

[List specially prepared for *The Londoner's Almanac* by Ellis Hillman, co-author with Richard Trench of *London Under London* (John Murray, 1985) and Chairman of the London Subterranean Survey Association. Information about the Association's work can be obtained from him, c/o North East London Polytechnic, Asta House, 156–164 High Road, Chadwell Heath, Romford, Essex, RM6 6LX.]

NATIONAL TRUST PROPERTIES IN LONDON

The National Trust owns 892 acres in London and holds 'protective covenants' over a further 26.5 acres [marked with *]. Only those marked 'P' are open to the public.

P*	Beulah Hill: Lawns Estate	P	Carlyle's House, 24 Cheyne Row, SW3
		*	3 Cheyne Walk, SW3
P	Blewcoat School, 23 Caxton Street, SW1 [now a National Trust shop and Information Centre]	*	93 Cheyne Walk, SW10
			97–100 Cheyne Walk, SW10

Chislehurst: Camden Court Land and Oak Bank Estate

* 32 and 34 Dartmouth Row, SE10

P Eastbury Manor House, Barking

P East Sheen Common

* 6 Eliot Place, SE3

P Fenton House, Windmill Hill, NW3

P George Inn, Borough High Street, SE1

P Ham House, Richmond [let to Department of the Environment]

P Hawkwood, between Chislehurst and Orpington

* The Hermitage, Enfield

33 Kensington Square, W8

P Osterley Park, Isleworth

P Petts Wood, between Chislehurst and Orpington

40, 42 and 44 Queen Anne's Gate, SW1 [the HQ of the National Trust]

P Rainham Hall, Rainham

P 'Roman' Bath, 5 Strand, WC2 [not open, but visible from path]

P Selsdon Wood

Squire's Mount, NW3

Sutton House, 2 & 4 Homerton High Street, E9

P Wandle Properties in the Colliers Wood/Mitcham/ Morden area, including Happy Valley, Merton Abbey Wall, Morden Hall, Wandle Park and Watermeade

LONDON'S TEN MOST POPULAR HISTORIC BUILDINGS [1984]

	Visitors		Visitors
St Paul's Cathedral	2–3 million*	Hampton Court Palace	554000
Westminster Abbey	2900000*	Palace of Westminster	144161
Tower of London	2340000	Kensington Palace	122000
Royal Botanic Gardens	1084291	The Monument	98700
		Forty Hall	83961
		Ham House	47078

Estimate

AN ARCHITECT'S-EYE VIEW OF THE BUILDINGS OF LONDON

TEN OF THE BEST

1 Renaissance building
The Banqueting House, Whitehall, SW1, 1619, by Inigo Jones.

2 Baroque interior
Christ Church Spitalfields, E1, 1714–29, by Nicholas Hawksmoor.

3 Architect's own house
Sir John Soane's Museum, 13 Lincoln's Inn Fields, WC2, 1812–34.

4 Nineteenth-century speculative development
Regent's Park, 1812–28, by John Nash and others.

5 Conservatory
The Palm House, Royal Botanic Gardens, Kew, 1844–48, by Decimus Burton and Richard Turner.

6 Nineteenth-century church
All Saints, Margaret Street, W1, 1849–59, by William Butterfield.

7 Nineteenth-century railway station and hotel
St Pancras, Euston Road, NW1, 1866–76, by Sir George Gilbert Scott.

8 Arts and crafts house
Swan House, 17 Chelsea Embankment, SW3, 1876, by R. Norman Shaw.

9 Post-war public building
Royal Festival Hall, South Bank, SE1, 1951, 1962, by Robert Matthew, J. Leslie Martin, Edwin Williams and Peter Moro.

10 Post-war office building
Economist Building, 25 St James's Street, SW1, 1960–64, by Alison and Peter Smithson.

TEN MOST SADLY MISSED

1 Medieval city
The City of London; burnt 1666.

2 Eighteenth-century speculative development
Adelphi, Strand, by the Adam Brothers, 1768–72; demolished 1937.

3 Prison
Newgate Prison, City, 1769, by George Dance the Younger; demolished 1902.

4 Nineteenth-century bridge
Old Waterloo Bridge, by George Rennie, 1811–17; demolished 1934.

5 Interiors
Bank of England banking halls, by Sir John Soane, 1798–1824; demolished 1924–39.

6 Post office
General Post Office, by Sir Robert Smirke, 1824–29; demolished 1912.

7 Nineteenth-century speculative development
Quadrant and Regent's Street, by John Nash, 1820s; demolished 1921–27.

8 Propylaeum
Euston Arch, Euston Station, by Philip Hardwick, 1834–38; demolished 1962.

9 Warehouses
St Katharine's Dock, 1836; partly demolished 1970s.

10 Cast-iron buildings
Coal Exchange, Monument Street, by J. B. Bunning, 1846–49; demolished 1962.

TEN LEAST LOVED

1 Housing estate
Barbican Estate, City, 1959–79, by Chamberlain, Powell & Bon.

2 Hotel
London Hilton, Park Lane, W1, 1963, by Lewis Solomon, Kaye and Partners.

3 Office block
Centrepoint, New Oxford Street, WC2, 1963–67, by Richard Siefert and Partners.

4 Culture complex
Hayward Gallery and Queen Elizabeth Hall, South Bank, SE1, 1964, by LCC/GLC Architects Department.

5 Government offices
Department of the Environment, Marsham Street, SW1, 1965–69, by Property Services Agency.

6 Army barracks
Household Cavalry Barracks, Knightsbridge, SW1, 1967–69, by Sir Basil Spence and Partners.

7 Park
Robin Hood Gardens, Poplar, E14, 1968–72, by Alison and Peter Smithson.

8 More government offices
Home Office, Petty France, SW1, 1970–73, by Sir Basil Spence and Partners.

9 More culture
Barbican Arts Centre, EC2, 1975–83, by Chamberlain, Powell & Bon.

10 Bank
National Westminster Tower, Old Broad Street, EC2, 1981, by Richard Siefert & Partners.

[Lists specially prepared for *The Londoner's Almanac* by Christopher Woodward, architect and lecturer at University College, London. He was co-author with Edward Jones of *A Guide to the Architecture of London* (Weidenfeld & Nicolson, 1983) which won the London Tourist Board Award for the Best London Guide Book.]

FLOODLIT LONDON BUILDINGS,

During the summer months (May to October) the Department of the Environment organizes the floodlighting of a number of important London buildings, including:

Admiralty Arch	Old Admiralty Building
Albert Memorial	Old War Office Building

Apsley House

British Museum

Dover House, Whitehall
(Scottish Office)

Gwydyr House, Whitehall
(Welsh Office)

Horseguards Building,
Whitehall

Houses of Parliament
(St Stephen's Tower,
Clock and Victoria
Tower; Terrace only
during summer recess)

Jewel Tower,
Westminster Abbey

Marble Arch

Middlesex Guildhall,
Broad Sanctuary, SW1

National Gallery

Natural History Museum

Norman Shaw Building,
Victoria Embankment
– formerly New
Scotland Yard (North)

Royal Courts of Justice

Royal Hospital, Chelsea
(Clock Tower and
Portico)

Royal Naval College,
Greenwich (for
certain functions
only)

St James's Park (Duck
Island, Bridge,
Fountains and Island
nearest Buckingham
Palace)

Somerset House

Tate Gallery

Trafalgar Square
(Nelson's Column and
Fountains)

Tower of London

Victoria and Albert
Museum

Wellington Barracks
(facing Birdcage
Walk)

BEVIS HILLIER'S TEN FAVOURITE ART DECO BUILDINGS IN GREATER LONDON

1 The Hoover Factory, Western Avenue, Perivale, W3
By Wallis, Gilbert and Partners, 1932–35. An extravaganza of
Egyptian and Aztec motifs with faïence decoration. It was
hated by the purists of the *Architectural Review* in the 1930s,
who called it 'façadist'. After this rude review came out it was
said that one of the Partners visited the *Review* office with a

horsewhip, thirsting for revenge – but fortunately the editor was out.

2 Park Lane Hotel, Piccadilly, W1
The steel skeleton of the building took so long to put up that taxi drivers nicknamed it 'the birdcage'. Its interior is sumptuous and largely unspoilt – the lamps are especially fine. Its chief glory is the Ballroom where the Prince of Wales used to dance with Gertie Lawrence and Mrs Simpson.

3 Jules's Bar, Jermyn Street, SW1
I don't know who designed it, and I have never patronized it as a 'regular' (the lure of the nearby 1970s Ritz Casino being so strong) but it is a perfect miniature of the more 'streamlined' type of Art Deco design that for me conjures up images of illicit meetings of Bright Young People, the *dramatis personae* of Michael Arlen's *Green Hat*.

4 Boulestin's Restaurant, Henrietta Street, WC2
Marcel Boulestin who opened this restaurant was so famous for his omelettes that he made a record explaining how to make them. The place used to have an exotic bar with glass pendants and wall paintings by Marie Laurencin and Laboureur – all now sadly removed. However, the flavour of this subterranean restaurant has survived its ritzing up in French Provincial style. Note especially the elaborate 1920s chandeliers which an artist I took there once described as 'like micro-photographs of malaria infestations'.

5 Daily Express building, Fleet Street, EC4
The shiny black exterior was once called 'a gentleman's bathroom turned inside out'. The wonderfully flashy entrance hall was, surprisingly, designed by Robert Atkinson, who also designed folksy holiday cottages in Cornwall for Sir John Betjeman's father, Ernest. The building still looks assertively and uncompromisingly modern after fifty years.

6 Head Office, Hay's Wharf, SE1
A bold and cheerful building on the Thames by Goodhart-

Rendel – a wealthy dilettante and musician better known for his writings on architecture than for his actual buildings (he was one of the first great enthusiasts for Victoriana). He had a sardonic wit: when in Athens with Osbert Lancaster, he circumnavigated the Parthenon and commented, 'Well! Not what you'd call an *unqualified* success, is it?' Dismissed by at least one modern architectural writer as a *flâneur*, Hay's Wharf shows what he could do when he meant business. The quirky gold lettering gives a lift to the heart as one floats past on a pleasure-boat.

7   Gentlemen's hairdressing salon, Austin Reed's, Regent Street, S W 1

Again, not somewhere I patronize personally (may I recommend Maurice in the Piccadilly Hotel barber's shop, with a gin and tonic afterwards in the big bar in Norman Shaw's 1904 building?). I include it, though, as something recherché (i.e. to show off that I know it at all!) but also as an example of the most hard-edge, cubist, non-decadent Deco. The chromium trim is as smart as the one you get in the barber's chair.

8   Ideal House, Great Marlborough Street, W 1

By Hood and Jeeves, 1928. It has the same all-black look as the *Express* building, but here the relief is in 'American Indian' type coloured tiling. Pretty successful attempts have been made to ruin it in modern times: the only good result is that the designer Bernard Nevill was able to lay his hands on some of the tile surrounds, and once generously offered to lend them to me for an exhibition in Minneapolis, Minnesota – which would have been returning Indian art to Indian territory. Unfortunately, it proved too expensive to ship them across the Atlantic.

9   Battersea Power Station, S W 8

By S. L. Pearce (engineer) and J. H. Halliday (architect) with Sir Giles Gilbert Scott (consulting architect), 1930–32. Yes, it *does* look rather like an upturned billiard table, but as you pass it on the train from Brighton to Victoria (or, more enjoyably, vice versa), the relativity of speed gives the illusion of some strange four-funnelled ocean liner. You can't criticize such a building on aesthetic criteria alone: think first of the problems for which it was a practical solution. Here Scott is as monolithic as the Pyramids, so it is odd to think that in the 1930s he also designed those telephone boxes that resemble latticed red sedan chairs.

10 High Point I Flats, North Road, Highgate, N6

By Lubetkin and Tecton. Because the Tecton Partnership also designed the Penguin Pool and Gorilla House at London Zoo, snide jokes are made by the reactionary school of modern architectural historians, who remark that 'their clients could not complain'. But High Point, though purist and extremist to the point of humourlessness, is a beautiful building (part of it was chosen for the cover of the 1979 Hayward Gallery *Thirties* exhibition catalogue), and I would be only too happy to live there. I believe architectural taste should be catholic enough to embrace both the rather show-off Jazz Age decoration of the Hoover Factory AND the 'architectural nudism' of High Point I. Those who take sides dogmatically miss so much.

[List specially prepared for *The Londoner's Almanac* by Bevis Hillier, the author of many books on the decorative arts, who was at the forefront of the modern revival of interest in Art Deco. After a number of years working for *The Times* and *Sunday Times*, and as editor of *The Connoisseur*, he has taken up an appointment with the *Los Angeles Times*. Having compiled this list – virtually his last endeavour before leaving England – he added: 'It has been *very* hard making a choice. My main regret is that no cinema goes in. If one did, it would be the marvellous geometric Muswell Hill Odeon, the first London building which made me enthusiastic about Art Deco.']

LONDON ON THE MOVE: TEN BITS OF LONDON THAT AREN'T WHERE THEY USED TO BE

Not all of London has ended up where its originators intended. Apart from the many buildings and architectural features that have been destroyed, a large number of the capital's monuments have been moved – sometimes to unlikely new locations. Here are the stories of ten of them:

1 Temple Bar

An elaborate arched structure, Temple Bar once stood in Fleet Street and marked the western junction between London and the City. In addition to its architectural interest (it was designed in 1672 by Sir Christopher Wren), it served the grisly purpose of displaying the heads of traitors which could be viewed through hired telescopes. By 1878 it had become an obstacle to traffic and was demolished. Ten years later it was erected on a private estate, Theobalds Park, Cheshunt, Hertfordshire. A long controversy has raged ever since as to its fate, and it has now been decided that it should be restored and re-erected in the churchyard of Wren's greatest building, St Paul's Cathedral. Parts of the various other City Gates [see page 140] have also been dispersed: four large stone griffin's heads from Bishopsgate now reside on the lawn of Wallington, Northumbria.

2 London Bridge

One of London's most famous sights, appropriately commemorated in the nursery rhyme, 'London Bridge is Falling Down', it was rebuilt several times between the Roman occupation and the nineteenth century when Sir John Rennie's five-arched stone bridge was constructed (1823–31). When this became inadequate for modern traffic, it was replaced (1967–72) by the present structure. Rennie's bridge was sold for £1 million to the developers of Lake Havasu City, Arizona. Shipped out stone by stone, each of them numbered, it was rebuilt and has become the principal tourist attraction of the region. If the rumour that its purchasers thought they were getting Tower Bridge is true, they have had the last laugh: Lake Havasu City is one of the most successful property developments in the USA.

3 Old London Bridge

When Rennie's London Bridge was built, many parts of the much-rebuilt medieval bridge were reused elsewhere. Two of the alcoves can be seen in Victoria Park, Hackney (which also has a Chinese pagoda, originally exhibited in Knightsbridge in 1847) and one is built into the fabric of Guy's Hospital. Stones from one of the arches (rediscovered in 1921) were incorporated into Adelaide House, King William Street, and a stone heraldic shield was used at Merstham Church, Surrey. The iron railings are now at St Botolph's churchyard, Bishopsgate, and there are houses such as 49 Heathfield Road, SW18 (and the wall outside Nos. 49–73) and in places as far afield as Herne Bay that can claim to have been built from stone salvaged from the bridge.

4 St Mary the Virgin Aldermanbury

One of the most dramatic re-siting operations ever carried out, this church – which Shakespeare probably visited and where John Milton was married – was rebuilt by Wren after the Great Fire and was gutted by an incendiary bomb on 29 December 1940. It stood a tragic ruin for 25 years until it was decided to dismantle it and ship all 7000 stones of it to the United States. There it was meticulously rebuilt (1965–69) as a memorial to Winston Churchill at Westminster College, Fulton, Missouri – where Churchill had made his famous 'Iron Curtain' speech in 1946. This building and London Bridge are not the only London monuments to have crossed the Atlantic; the catalogue includes the bells from the war-damaged St Dunstan in the East, which are now in a vineyard in California's Napa Valley, an angel from St Bride's Church which is now in the University of Southern Illinois and the font from All-Hallows by the Tower which now resides in Christ Church, Philadelphia. Fraternal post-war gifts of this kind can perhaps be better understood than the presence of a lamp from the old Waterloo Bridge that has ended up in Harare, Zimbabwe (formerly Salisbury, Rhodesia) or the railings from St Paul's Cathedral that were ripped out in 1874 and are now in Toronto!

5 Wellington statue

A 40-ton bronze equestrian statue depicting the Duke of Wellington on his horse Copenhagen, was unveiled at Hyde Park Corner in 1846. In 1883, when the arch on which it was sited was moved to Constitution Hill, this much-criticized statue (known as the 'Arch Duke') was removed to its present location, Round Hill, Aldershot.

6 Mercer's Hall frontage

Mercer's Hall in Ironmonger Lane was rebuilt after the Great Fire and acquired a new façade in 1879, at which time the old façade was dismantled and taken to Swanage where it forms part of the Town Hall. The contractor who undertook this work was also responsible for other building in Swanage, which explains the mysterious presence of bollards marked 'City of London'. (The 'recycling' of parts of demolished London buildings has been quite commonplace; among the most notable is the portico of the National Gallery where the architect William Wilkins was compelled to incorporate the Corinthian columns from Carlton House which was demolished in 1828. Other columns were used in the Chapel at Buckingham Palace. The gates from Cremorne Gardens became the entrance to a brewery in Tetcott Road, SW10, and Brunel, when rebuilding Hungerford Bridge, made use of the chains in his Clifton Suspension Bridge.)

7 All Hallows tower

The tower of All Hallows, Lombard Street – the Wren church where John Wesley preached his first sermon – demolished in 1938–39, was rebuilt as the tower of All Hallows, North Twickenham. The church also contains the older All Hallows' furniture and most of its monuments. Its fabric also incorporates the porch from the Priory of St John, Clerkenwell.

8 Seven Dials obelisk

At the junction of seven streets in the area between Soho and Covent Garden, an obelisk was erected in the 1690s, surmounted by a clock with seven faces – hence the name. The area became a notorious haunt of criminals and, in 1773, in the erroneous belief that treasure was buried beneath it, vandals tore it up. After languishing for some years in a stonemason's yard in Chertsey, in 1822 it was erected on the Green in Weybridge, Surrey. There has been a recent move to reinstate it in London.

9 St Antholin's spire

Regarded as one of Wren's greatest churches, St Antholin was tragically demolished in 1875 to make way for the building of

Queen Victoria Street. All that remains of this magnificent church, the top part of the spire, is now in the gardens of a club in Forest Hill.

10 Charles II statue

A statue of Charles II on horseback, trampling Oliver Cromwell beneath the horse's hooves, was said to have been commissioned originally as a representation of King John Sobieski of Poland crushing a Turk. It was acquired by Sir Robert Vyner and erected in 1672 at the Stocks Market. When, in 1738, this area was cleared for the building of the Mansion House, the statue was removed and resided in a builder's yard until 1779 when a descendant of Vyner took it to Gautby Park, Lincolnshire. From there, in 1883, it was moved to Newby Hall, Yorkshire. It is now in Ripon. Not only is it one of London's most travelled statues; it is also one of the strangest, for although the sculptor altered the Polish king's head to that of Charles II, the recumbent victim, supposed to be Cromwell, is still wearing a turban.

THE CONTENTS OF CLEOPATRA'S NEEDLE 'TIME CAPSULE'

'Time capsules' – receptacles containing objects representing the age in which they are buried – have been placed beneath many notable London buildings, including Waterloo Bridge in 1939 and Lloyds in 1984.

Cleopatra's Needle, a stone obelisk dating from about 1475 BC, was transported to London and erected on the Victoria Embankment in 1878. The bizarre list of contents of its time capsule, in two earthenware containers, includes:

* A bronze half inch to a foot scale model of the obelisk

* A piece of granite chipped from it

* A complete set of British currency and one Indian rupee (Queen Victoria had been made Empress of India in 1876)

* A standard foot, pound, two-foot rule and standard gauge for measuring to 1/1000th of an inch

* A portrait of Queen Victoria

* A box of hairpins

* Copies of various books, including a *London Directory*, *Whitaker's Almanac*, *Bradshaw's Railway Guide* and copies of the Bible in various languages, the Pentateuch in Hebrew and Book of Genesis in Arabic

* A map of London

* A parchment copy of Samuel Birch's translation of the Needle's hieroglyphics

* A selection of daily and weekly newspapers

* Copies of *Engineering* magazine printed on vellum

* Doulton jars

* A shilling 'Mappin's Sculling Razor'

* A box of cigars and a pipe

* An 'Alexandra' feeding bottle and toys

* A Tangye's hydraulic jack

* Iron ropes and submarine cables

* Portraits of twelve of the prettiest Englishwomen

TEN FACTS ABOUT BIG BEN

1   The origin of the name of London's most famous landmark is uncertain. It derives either from Chief Commissioner of Works, Sir Benjamin Hall, or possibly from the 18-stone boxer, Benjamin Caunt.

2   The Great Bell was damaged when it was dropped on the deck of the schooner on which it was being transported from Stockton-on-Tees to London in 1856. An over-weight clapper caused a 4-ft crack and necessitated recasting at a foundry in Whitechapel. It entered service on 31 May 1859 but cracked again in September, though repairs enabled its continued use ever since. It weighs 13.5 tons, is 9 ft in diameter and 7.5 ft high. It was hoisted into position with a chain 1600 ft long.

3   The 5-ton clock represents the first use of a 'double three-legged gravity escapement' to protect the 6-cwt pendulum from environmental influences such as wind pressure.

4   The timing is maintained with old pennies; adding one to the balance results in a 2/5 of a second gain in 24 hours.

5   The chime is derived from a phrase by Handel in accompaniment to the aria, 'I know that my Redeemer liveth' from *Messiah*.

6   There have been several stoppages including intentional ones during 1916 when all public clocks were silenced from sunset to sunrise in anticipation of German Zeppelins homing in on them; in 1944 it stopped twice – once when a workman left a hammer inside the mechanism and once when a spring broke; in 1945 the hammer mechanism froze, preventing it from striking; in 1949 the hands were stopped by swarming starlings. The longest stoppage, of 13 days, during repairs, was in 1977.

7   The clock was wound by hand until 1913. It took two men 32 hours once a week.

8   The Ayrton light in the lantern indicates that parliament is in session.

9   There are 336 stairs to the belfry.

10   The chimes were first broadcast on the radio in 1923 and on television in 1949.

London's Seven City Gates

In c200 AD the Romans built a wall round the area roughly corresponding to the City of London. It was about 3 miles long and enclosed 330 acres. Sections of the wall can still be seen; the Ordnance Survey map, *Londonium*, is the best guide to the line of the wall and to existing features, and there is a model in the Museum of London. All the gates piercing the wall were demolished in the 1760s and few traces can be seen today, although all are recalled in the names of nearby streets. Running clockwise, the gates were:

1 Ludgate
Traditionally named after the mythical King Lud, but almost certainly Roman, it once contained a prison. Statues of Queen Elizabeth and 'King Lud' and his two sons that once stood on the gate are now at St Dunstan in the West, Fleet Street.

2 Newgate
The gate to the road to Silchester and the West, rebuilt several times – once under a bequest of Dick Whittington, the Lord Mayor. It was demolished in 1767, the last of the City gates to disappear.

3 Aldersgate
The gate on the road joining Watling Street, perhaps named after someone called 'Ealdred'. In a room above it John Day, the leading printer of Queen Elizabeth I's reign, produced many notable works. On 20 October 1660 Samuel Pepys recorded in his *Diary* seeing the limbs of traitors displayed on Aldersgate.

4 Cripplegate
Perhaps named after the cripples who once begged there, this was the gate through which Elizabeth I first entered London in 1558.

5 Moorgate

Probably a postern gate in the City wall added after the Roman period, it was demolished in 1762 and materials from it used to shore up the crumbling fabric of London Bridge.

6 Bishopsgate

The gate leading to the North via Ermine Street, it received its name in Saxon times; the Bishop of London could once claim one stick from every wagonload of wood passing through it.

7 Aldgate

Aldgate provided access to the road to Colchester and the East. Geoffrey Chaucer lived in a room above it from 1374 to 1385; it was later rebuilt and used as a school. When it was finally demolished, some of the stones were shipped to Northumberland and used in the building of Rothley Castle.

A GEOLOGIST'S FAVOURITE BUILDINGS

Dr J. Eric Robinson, Senior Lecturer in the Department of Geology at University College, London, and the author of *London: Illustrated Geological Walks*, Book One: The City; Book Two: The West End (Scottish Academic Press, 1984), offers a novel view of London from the point of view of the geologist. From this perspective, his ten favourite buildings are:

1 The Roman city wall

A good example is the rounded corner bastion close to St Giles without Cripplegate church, Fore Street, EC2. The wall is buff-coloured Kentish Rag from the Medway, with fragments of red tile and assorted rubble added locally.

2   St Paul's Cathedral

A monument to the enduring qualities of Portland Stone after three centuries of weathering. A geological bonus must be the Victorian additions to the West Front, particularly the steps and paving which introduce many different rock types.

3   The Albert Memorial, Kensington Gardens, SW7

A combination of stones, selected for their colour and texture to achieve the 'jewel' effect of the whole. The memorial combines granites from the Mourne Mountains, Mull and Cornwall. The paving is of North Wales Slate, New Red Sandstone and Portland Stone (black, pink and white respectively). The sculptural friezes [see also *The Albert Memorial*, p. 59] are of Carrara Marble, variously weathered and stained.

4   Natural History Museum, Cromwell Road, SW7

Built entirely of terracotta blocks, a favourite material of nineteenth-century architects, especially Alfred Waterhouse. The fine clay paste could be moulded to any shape, and then fired to high temperatures to produce three-dimensional sculptural units of near-permanent life span. The surface of the building is encrusted with terracotta models of prehistoric beasts which portray the state of palaeontological knowledge a century ago.

5   St Pancras Station, Euston Road, NW1

It has similar attributes to those of the Albert Memorial, with the added interest that the architect, Sir George Gilbert Scott, appears to have incorporated into its fabric many of the building stones worked in the regions served by the Midland Railway for whom the Station and Hotel were built. Red granites from Peterhead and Shap are prominent against a structure mainly of red Nottinghamshire brick. Buff stone dressings come from Stamford and Mansfield, while the curving steps are from the West Riding of Yorkshire.

6   The Baltic Exchange, St Mary Axe, EC3
Built 1900–03, this robust commercial trading post shows the quality of polished granite. Appropriately, the stone is a rich red rock from Sweden – Virgo Granite; the solid blocks and columns (no mere cladding this) retain a mirror-like polish. The interiors are richly panelled with the strongly coloured marbles which were so popular in Edwardian times.

7   The Economist building, 25 St James's Street, SW1
Here there is agreement between geologist and architectural historian over Alison and Peter Smithson's 1964 building which has won widespread praise. The ingenious towers, steps and ramps set into the conventions of St James's are geologically exciting for the use of highly fossiliferous Portland Roach – a shelly version of conventional Portland Stone from the same Dorset quarries. A fossil-hunter's delight.

8   Euston Station, Euston Road, NW1
Having bemoaned the loss of the Euston Arch (Bramley Falls Sandstone from Leeds) along with the Victorian Society, a resounding cheer for British Rail for the new black towers of Euston. Here we have the largest surface area of Bushveld Gabbro to be seen anywhere outside the Transvaal, and all of it is highly polished so we can see its crystal textures.

9   National Westminster tower, 25 Old Broad Street, EC2
Like a captive Apollo rocket, but with an extensive launching pad fully clad in highly polished natural stones. To Bishopsgate, the walls are lined with silver-grey Sardinian Granite from Sassari. The inner base to the tower is faced with grain-patterned red-brown Dakota Mahogany Granite from the Mid-West of North America. All surfaces deserve close scrutiny to appreciate minerals and crystal textures. The interiors, flooring and walling are of Italian Perlato Marble from Sicily.

10   Ismaili Centre, 1 Cromwell Gardens, SW7
Something of a geological jewel set within a district of Victorian character – an Arab tent in stone. The Muslim holy colours, blue and white, are achieved through the use of Sardinian Grey Granite, which comprises the bulk of the building, with the narrow window surroundings picked out in deep blue stone – Blue Bahia Syenite from Brazil.

TEN LONDON STONES

The historical associations of these stones evoke far more than their humble appearance suggests:

1   The Stone of Scone, Westminster Abbey
This famous holy relic is said to be the stone on which Jacob laid his head as he dreamed, and was the coronation stone of Scottish kings. It was captured from the Scots in 1296 by Edward I and incorporated into his Coronation Chair – on which almost all subsequent monarchs have been crowned. It was stolen in 1950 but later recovered.

2   The Rosetta Stone, British Museum
Discovered in Egypt in 1799 and brought to England in 1802, it has text in Egyptian hieroglyphics, demotic Egyptian and Greek and enabled hieroglyphics to be deciphered for the first time by Jean François Champollion and other scholars.

3   London Stone, Cannon Street, EC4
Said to be the milestone from which the Romans measured all the distances in the province, its antiquity has been much disputed.

4   Whittington Stone, Highgate Hill, N19
Erected in 1821 on the site of a much older wayside cross, it is
reputed to mark the site where Dick Whittington stood when
he heard Bow bells calling him back to be 'thrice Lord Mayor
of London'.

5   Wellington Stones, Athenaeum Club, Pall Mall, SW1
These two slabs were erected when the Club was opened in
1830 to enable the Duke of Wellington to mount his horse.

6   Tyburn Stone, 195 Edgware Road, W2
A stone gatepost of one of the three toll gates from nearby
Tyburn, once the main venue for public hangings, is now
displayed in the window of Lloyds Bank.

7   'Long Meg', Westminster Abbey
A large blue stone set in the South Walk of the Abbey, it was
thought to mark the grave of a giantess who lived in the time of
Henry VIII, but it is probably the tombstone of twenty-six
monks who died in the Black Death.

8   Hyde Park Standing Stone
In The Dell to the east of the Serpentine there is a 7-ton slab
reputed to have been taken from Stonehenge by Charles I. In
fact, although it was imported (from Cornwall) it is part of a
drinking fountain set up in 1861 and later demolished.

9   Holocaust Garden Stone
In Hyde Park, east of the Serpentine and facing the Standing
Stone, it commemorates the victims of the Holocaust.

10   Norwegian Navy Stone
On the north side of the Serpentine, it was presented by the
Norwegian Navy in 1978 in gratitude for aid given by the
British in the Second World War.

THE COADE STONE MYSTERY

A type of terracotta originally made in Lambeth in the early eighteenth century was later in the century improved by the Coade family – especially through the business acumen of Eleanor Coade. Coade Stone was as easily worked as clay, but once hardened had extraordinary resistance to weathering and was widely used in London for elaborate decorative features typical of the age. When the Coade Artificial Stone Manufactory closed in 1840, the secret process was lost and has never been rediscovered. There are innumerable examples of the use of Coade Stone in London, such as:

1 Cherubs on the wall of the Norwegian Embassy, 25 Belgrave Square, 1776.
2 Twenty-nine vases on the parapet of Somerset House, Strand, 1787.
3 Figures of Tritons on the Admiralty, Whitehall, 1788.
4 The frieze by John Flaxman at the Royal Opera House, Covent Garden, depicting Tragedy and Comedy, 1808.
5 Relief (1810–13) on the west pediment of Greenwich Palace, designed by Benjamin West.
6 The tomb of Captain Bligh (d.1817), and other monuments at St Mary's Church, Lambeth.
7 The caryatids of St Pancras Church, Euston Road (1819–22) by John Rossi.
8 Figures of a boy and girl in the former churchyard of St Botolph, Bishopsgate, one of which is dated 1821.
9 The so-called 'Coade Lion' (1837) on the south side of Westminster Bridge – formerly at the entrance to the Lion Brewery.
10 Statues of 'Europe', 'Asia', 'Africa' and 'America' for the Bank of England, 1801.

THE TEN MOST IMPORTANT ARCHAEOLOGICAL FINDS IN LONDON

1 Acheulian flint hand-axe
c100000 BC
British Museum

Found c1690 by John Conyers in what is now King's Cross Road with 'the body of an elephant' – evidently the bones of a mammoth. The first recorded find of a Palaeolithic tool associated with an extinct animal.

2 Battersea Shield
Early 1st century AD
British Museum

Recovered from the Thames at Battersea, 1857. Made of bronze with red glass inlay, the Shield represents the finest example of a Pre-Roman Celtic tradition of bronze working. It was probably deposited deliberately in the river as a votive offering.

3 Tombstone of Classicianus
Some time after AD 61
British Museum

The two inscribed fragments of this great funerary monument of C. Julius Classicianus were found separately in 1852 and 1935 on Tower Hill. We know from the Roman historian Tacitus that Classicianus, as Procurator (financial controller), was responsible for preventing excessive revenge from being exacted on the defeated tribes that took part in the revolt of Boudicca (Boadicea), the native British queen, against the Roman administration, AD 60–61.

4 Bronze head of the Emperor Hadrian
cAD 122
British Museum

The Emperor visited Britain and presumably London in AD 122, and it is possible that this impressive imperial statue was set up to commemorate this visit. At some later date, perhaps in the 4th or 5th century, the head was hacked from the body and thrown into the Thames near London Bridge, from where it was recovered in 1834.

5 Marble head of the god Mithras
Late 2nd – early 3rd century, AD
Museum of London

Probably from a bull-slaying group, the rest of which may have been in stucco. The head has been struck on the left side of the neck with an axe, and was broken into two pieces. These were carefully buried in a late floor of the Walbrook Mithraeum, at the junction of Queen Victoria Street and Walbrook, with other sculptures during the first half of the 4th century, perhaps after an abortive attack which moved the Mithraists to hide their treasures. It was found during excavations in 1954.

6 Dowgate Hill Brooch
10th century
British Museum

A Saxon gold brooch of outstanding quality. It is decorated with gold filigree, four inset pearls and an enamelwork portrait – perhaps of the owner. It was recovered from the Thames foreshore in 1839.

7 Viking tombstone
Early 11th century
Museum of London

A carved stone slab found in 1852 on the south side of St Paul's churchyard at a depth of 8 metres. It probably formed one end of a sarcophagus. The stone is carved in Anglo-Saxon 'Ring-erike' style and shows a stylized lion fighting a serpent. The stone was originally painted and has on its left edge a runic inscription in Old Norse.

8   The Walbrook coin hoard
Mostly 11th century
Museum of London; British Museum;
Ashmolean Museum, Oxford

A hoard of some 7000 coins, including three foreign coins, deposited c1070; perhaps a 'bullion' store of a London moneyer, hidden for safety and awaiting conversion into current coin after the Conquest. The hoard was recovered in secrecy in 1872 and subsequently split up and sold.

9   Foster Lane glass
First half of 14th century
Museum of London

Recovered from a chalk-lined cess-pit during development in 1982. Some 50 fragments of thin, colourless glass decorated with brilliant red, blue, green, yellow and white enamel heraldic designs and mottoes. Six, perhaps eight, beakers were thrown away together. They belong to a rare group of medieval glass vessels probably made either in Syrian glass-houses to European order, or in Europe with skills learnt from Syria.

10   Cheapside Hoard
Probably buried 1603
Museum of London; Victoria and Albert Museum

A large hoard of Jacobean jewellery, probably part of the stock of a goldsmith living in Cheapside. Found in a box beneath a floor in 1912, the hoard had perhaps been buried for safety during an outbreak of the plague in 1603 and never recovered. This fabulous collection includes cameos, intaglios, enamelled rings, rings with faceted gems, hair pins, hat badges, ruby and diamond buttons, and 'carcanets' or looped gold chains.

[List specially prepared for *The Londoner's Almanac* by Hugh Chapman, Deputy Director, and Brian Hobley, Chief Urban Archaeologist, The Museum of London.]

THE TEN MOST SPECTACULAR JEWELS ON DISPLAY IN LONDON

1   The Canning Jewel (Victoria and Albert Museum)
A merman with the jawbone of an ass in one hand and a Medusa-head shield in the other. His naked torso is convincingly formed by a large baroque pearl, and the rest is of enamelled gold, set with rubies and diamonds. It is probably Italian, dating from c1600. It was brought from India by Lord Canning after the Mutiny of 1857–59.

2   The Stuart Sapphire (Tower of London)
Probably the stone worn by George Neville, Archbishop of York, in his mitre and confiscated by Edward IV. It descended through the royal family and was taken into exile by James II, who reputedly always carried it in his pocket. It returned to England and was sold from among Cardinal York's effects to George IV. It is now set in the back of the Imperial State Crown.

3   The Black Prince's Ruby (Tower of London)
It is actually not a true ruby, but a large uncut spinel or balas ruby. It was given by Pedro the Cruel, Grandee of Castile, to the Black Prince in 1367, and was supposedly worn by Henry V in the crown on his helmet at the Battle of Agincourt. It was later set in Charles II's State Crown, and prominently in every state crown since then, including the present Imperial State Crown.

4   The Koh-i-Nur (Mountain of Light) (Tower of London)
This has two legends attached to it: one is that its owner rules the world, the other, that it is unlucky for any but a woman to wear it. Its history goes back to the fourteenth century. It later passed into the hands of the Mogul empress and was supposedly given by Shah Jehan to his wife, Mumtaz. Reputedly once of 1000 carats, it was reduced by cutting to 186.5. In 1739 it was captured by Nadir Shah and taken back to Persia. The desire to possess it led to many torturings and blindings of its

temporary owners. It passed into Sikh hands and was captured by the British when the Punjab was annexed. The East India Company presented it to Queen Victoria who had it recut to its present size, 106.5 carats. It is set in the crown of Queen Elizabeth, the Queen Mother. In deference to the legend, no king of England has ever worn it.

5   The Cullinan Diamond (Tower of London)
A 3106 carat diamond named after Thomas Cullinan, President of De Beers. Given to King Edward VII on his birthday in 1907 by the government of the Transvaal, it was split into four main parts and some lesser stones:

THE STAR OF AFRICA, a pearshape of 530 carats, set in the head of the Royal Sceptre.

THE SECOND STAR OF AFRICA, a square of 317 carats, set in the front of the Imperial State Crown, under the Black Prince's Ruby.

THE THIRD STAR OF AFRICA, a pearshape of 95 carats, set in the mould of Queen Mary's Crown.

THE FOURTH STAR OF AFRICA, a heartshape of 64 carats, set in the cross at the top of Queen Mary's Crown.

6   The Gatacre Jewel (Victoria and Albert Museum)
An amethyst carved with the head of Medusa in late Roman times and set in an enamelled gold frame c1550. It belonged to the Gatacre family of Shropshire and was romantically known as the 'Fair Maid of Gatacre' after Joan (born 1509), the daughter of Robert Gatacre.

7   The Armada Jewel (Victoria and Albert Museum)
Enamelled gold, set with rubies and diamonds and enclosing a portrait relief of Queen Elizabeth I, a painted portrait of her by Nicholas Hilliard and emblematic allusions to her. According to tradition, the jewel was given by Elizabeth to Sir Thomas Heneage after the defeat of the Spanish Armada in 1588.

152

8 The Lyte Jewel (British Museum – Waddesdon Bequest)
Enamelled gold, set with rubies and diamonds and enclosing a
portrait miniature of James I. Given by the King to Thomas
Lyte of Lyte's Cary, Somerset, in 1610. Lyte's portrait,
wearing this jewel, still survives.

9 The Dunstable Swan Jewel (British Museum)
A tiny gold swan, with white enamelled plumage, a gold crown
around its neck and on a chain. It was made around 1400 in
Paris or, less probably, in England. The swan was the badge of
the Bohun-Lancaster dynasty, and also a number of very
important European nobles such as the Duke of Berry, the
Duke of Cleves and the Margrave of Brandenburg. This little
jewel was found in an excavation at Dunstable in 1965.

10 The Chauncey Hare Townshend Star Sapphire
(Victoria and Albert Museum)
A very fine circular star sapphire surrounded by diamonds and
set in a ring. This is the most exceptional piece in a collection of
precious stones bequeathed to the Museum by the Rev.
Chauncey Hare Townshend (1798–1868), cleric and poet.

[List specially prepared for *The Londoner's Almanac* by Anna Somers Cocks, Assistant
Keeper at the Victoria and Albert Museum, organizer of the 'Princely Magnificence'
exhibition of Renaissance jewels and co-author of *Renaissance Jewels, Gilt Boxes and*
Objets de Vertu in the Thyssen-Bornemisza Collection (Philip Wilson, 1984).]

LONDON'S TEN OLDEST
OUTDOOR STATUES

1 c1600 BC
Statue of Sekhmet over Sotheby's, 34 Bond Street, W1.
Almost 150 years older than Cleopatra's Needle, it was unsold
at the Consul Salt sale of 1835 and has stayed at Sotheby's ever
since.

2 Late 14th century
Statue said to be King Alfred, formerly at Westminster Hall and in 1824 erected in Trinity Church Square, SE1.

3 1586
Queen Elizabeth I at the church of St Dunstan in the West, Fleet Street, EC4 – originally on Ludgate and moved here when it was demolished.

4 1633
Bronze equestrian statue of Charles I in Trafalgar Square. It has had a most colourful history. Made by Hubert Le Sueur, a Huguenot sculptor whose name can be seen on one of the horse's hooves, it was ordered to be destroyed during the Commonwealth. Instead, John Rivett, the contractor appointed to cut it up, buried it and sold souvenirs allegedly made from parts of it. At the Restoration, Charles II acquired it and set it up in Charing Cross. It was eventually moved to Trafalgar Square.

5 1668
Guy of Warwick's stone statue at the corner of Newgate Street and Warwick Lane, EC4 – on the site of his house.

6 1676
Robert Devereux, Earl of Essex – a bust above the Devereux Inn, Devereux Court, WC2.

7 1676
Charles II in bronze by Grinling Gibbons at Chelsea Hospital, SW3.

8 1681
Charles II by Caius Gabriel Cibber. The much-weathered statue, once owned by W. S. Gilbert, was set up in Soho Square, W1, in 1938.

9 1688

The so-called 'Pannier Boy' set up on 27 August 1688 in
Panyer Alley, EC4, depicts a boy with a panyer, or bread-
basket. It was removed for safe-keeping during the Second
World War and restored to the site in 1964.

10 1702

Henry VIII by Francis Bird, over the gateway of St Bartholemew's Hospital, EC1, which Henry re-founded in 1544.

TWENTY-SIX NUDE STATUES IN LONDON

There are many nude statues in London, some of which have
been the cause of considerable controversy: the statue of
Achilles, paid for 'by the women of England', was much
attacked (and its figleaf has been stolen several times); 'Aspiration' was originally totally nude, but a sporran was added
following complaints, and Epstein's 'Rima' has even been
tarred and feathered!

'Achilles' (1822) by Richard Westmacott, Park Lane, W1.

'Archimedes' (1962) by Edwin Russell, junction of Lombard
Road and York Road, SW11.

'Aspiration' (1959) by E. Bainbridge, 258 Edgware Road, W2.

'Atalanta' (1929) by Francis Derwent Wood, Cheyne Walk,
SW3.

'Beyond Tomorrow' (1972) by Karin Jonzen, Guildhall Yard,
EC2.

'Boy' (1902) by John MacAllen Swan, Dutch Garden, Holland
Park, W8.

'Boy with a Dolphin' (1975) by David Wynne, Pier House,
Oakley Street, SW3.

'Boy with Frog' fountain (1936) by Sir William Reid Dick, Queen Mary's Gardens, Regent's Park, NW1.

'La Deliverance' (1927) by Emile Guillaume, junction of Finchley Road and North Circular Road, NW11.

'The Eagle Slayer' (1851; erected 1927) by John Bell, Bethnal Green Museum, Cambridge Heath Road, E2.

'The Hammerthrower' (1973) by John Robinson, Tower Place, EC3.

'Horse and Rider' (1975) by Elizabeth Frink, corner of Piccadilly and Dover Street, W1.

'Hylas' (1933) by H. A. Pegram, Regent's Park lily pond, NW1.

'Joy of Life' (1963) by T. B. Huxley-Jones, opposite Grosvenor House Hotel, Park Lane, W1.

'The Lesson' (1958) by Franta Belsky, junction of Turin Street and Bethnal Green Road, E2.

'Lost Bow' (1939) by A. H. Hodge, Queen Mary's Gardens, Regent's Park, NW1.

'Mighty Hunter' (1939) by A. H. Hodge, Queen Mary's Gardens, Regent's Park, NW1.

Nude bronze of girl on cattle trough (1911), Anon., behind the Royal Exchange, EC3.

Nude fountain (c1858) by Alexander Monro, Berkeley Square, W1.

'Nude Man' (1952) by D. Wain-Hobson, forecourt of St James's Hospital, Sarsfield Road, SW12.

'Pan' (1961) by Sir Jacob Epstein, Bowater House, Edinburgh Gate, SW1.

'Paternoster – Shepherd and Sheep' (1975) by Elizabeth Frink, Paternoster Square, EC4.

'Pocahontas' (1956) by David McFall, formerly in Red Lion Square, WC1; moved inside lobby of Cassell & Co., Vincent Square, SW1.

'Rima' (1925) by Sir Jacob Epstein, north of the Serpentine, Hyde Park, W2.

'The Seer' (1957) by Gilbert Ledward, 197 Knightsbridge, SW1.

'The Sun Worshippers' (commenced 1910; erected 1980) by Sir Jacob Epstein, Kensington and Chelsea Town Hall, Hornton Street, W8.

Venus Fountain (1953) by Gilbert Ledward, Sloane Square, SW1.

STATUES OF FIVE AMERICANS

1   John Kennedy (1917–63), 34th President of the USA
1 Park Crescent, Marylebone Road, NW1
Bronze bust by Jacques Lipchitz, 1965.

2   Abraham Lincoln (1809–65), 16th President of the USA
Parliament Square, SW1
Copy of the Chicago, Illinois, statue by Augustus Saint-Gaudens, 1920.
Royal Exchange, EC3
Bust by Andrew O'Connor, 1930.

3   George Peabody (1795–1869), Philanthropist
Royal Exchange, EC3
Statue by W. W. Story, 1869.

4   Franklin Delano Roosevelt (1882–1945), 32nd President of the USA
Grosvenor Square, W1
Bronze by Sir William Reid Dick, 1948.

5   George Washington (1732–99), First President of the USA
Trafalgar Square, SW1
Copy of the Richmond, Virginia, statue by Jean-Antoine Houdon, 1921.

SOME STRANGE FACTS ABOUT LONDON'S STATUES

1   The memorial to Sir Walter Besant (1836–1901) on Victoria Embankment is the only outdoor representation in London of a person wearing spectacles.

2   No one knows the identity of the lead statue of a queen in Queen Square, WC1. It could be Queen Charlotte, Mary or Anne. The sculptor is also unknown.

3   Oliver Cromwell's statue outside Westminster Hall is wearing his spurs upside down.

4   When the statue of Earl Haig opposite the Banqueting Hall in Whitehall was unveiled in 1937, it started a long argument in *The Times*; not only were the horse's legs said to be incorrectly positioned, but Haig is depicted hatless – despite the fact that he is in uniform.

5   The statue of Sir Henry Havelock in Trafalgar Square, unveiled in 1861, was the first to be executed from a photograph.

6   The only statue in London with a facsimile of the subject's signature is that of Sir Thomas More outside Chelsea Old Church, Embankment.

7 Florence Nightingale was known as 'the lady with the lamp' – but the lamp she actually used was nothing like the Roman oil lamp her statue in Waterloo Place holds.

8 The statue of Sir Sydney Waterlow in Waterlow Park, N19 (and a copy in front of Westminster City School) is unique in London in that he carries an umbrella.

9 The paws of the lions in Trafalgar Square were modelled by Sir Edwin Landseer from those of a cat.

10 The 80 ft statue outside Thorn-EMI in St Martin's Lane, WC2, known as 'The Spirit of Electricity' has lights set into it to make it glow.

11 Almost all popular representations of 'Justice' – the statue on the Central Criminal Court, Old Bailey – depict her blindfolded; in fact, she is not.

12 George IV in Trafalgar Square is riding a horse without stirrups.

13 The ears of Handel in Westminster Abbey are not his own. The sculptor, Louis-François Roubiliac, thought them unfittingly large for the great composer and modelled them on those of a Miss Rich.

14 The caryatids supporting the portico of St Pancras Church, Euston Road, WC1, were too tall and a section had to be sliced out of their middles to make them fit.

TEN HOLY RELICS IN WESTMINSTER ABBEY

In the Middle Ages, Westminster Abbey was a major repository of 'Holy Relics', including:

Stones used for stoning St Stephen
Bones of the Holy Innocents
A tooth of one of the Magi
The girdle of the Virgin Mary
Hair of Mary Magdalene .

A phial of holy blood
A footprint of Christ in stone
A tooth of St Athanasius
The head of St Benedict
St Peter's vestments

Ten Saints with London Connections

1 Saint Mellitus, d.624

The first Bishop of London, consecrated in c604, and the founder of St Paul's Cathedral, Mellitus was a Roman abbot sent to England by St Gregory to aid St Augustine of Canterbury in the conversion of the English.

2 Saint Sebi, 664–694

Sebi, or Sebert, was King of the East Saxons in whose conversion he assisted. He was reputed to have built the first monastery at Westminster. He was buried in Old St Paul's, where he performed wonders even after his death: his first stone coffin was made too short, as was the second, but without giving the coffin-maker a chance at 'third time lucky', it miraculously lengthened.

3 Saint Wilgefortis, dates unknown

Also known by various other names, including Uncumber, legend had it that she was one of the septuplet daughters of the King of Portugal. Having taken a vow of chastity, she grew a beard to ward off her suitor, the King of Sicily. This so offended her father that he crucified her. Her name was evoked by women with troublesome husbands. Her effigy in the Henry VII chapel in Westminster Abbey was traditionally offered oats by worshippers – a bizarre custom much criticized by Thomas More.

4 Saint Dunstan, 909–988

Noted as a craftsman and musician, Dunstan was a Benedictine monk and reformer who restored monasticism to England after the Danish invasion. He became Archbishop of Canterbury in 959, obtained from King Edgar the charter that founded Westminster Abbey and was Bishop of London from 959–960.

5 Edward the Confessor, 1003–1066

Edward was the son of King Edgar. His reputation for holiness is based partly on his supposed ability to cure the disease, scrofula, known as the 'king's evil', with a touch, and partly because his marriage was allegedly unconsummated. He refounded and endowed Westminster Abbey, establishing it as the venue for the coronation and burial of English monarchs. His remains are in a shrine dedicated to him in the Abbey in 1268.

6 John Fisher, 1469–1535

The Bishop of Rochester, under Henry VIII John Fisher upheld the validity of the King's marriage to Catherine of Aragon and refused to take the oath of succession. In 1534 he was imprisoned in the Tower and while there was created a cardinal – which enraged the King. He was tried and executed in 1535 – he was so frail that he had to be carried to the block. His body was buried at All Hallows Barking (by the Tower) and later in St Peter ad Vincula in the Tower. His head, after being displayed on London Bridge, was thrown into the Thames. He was canonized in 1935.

7 Thomas More, 1478–1535

Henry VIII's Lord Chancellor and author of *Utopia*, like Fisher he refused to acknowledge the Act of Succession and was imprisoned in the Tower and executed in 1535. His body was buried in St Peter ad Vincula and his head in Canterbury. More is commemorated by a memorial and statue at Chelsea Old Church. He was canonized in 1935.

8 John Houghton, 1487–1533

Along with Fisher and More, Houghton, the Prior of Charter-house, refused to acknowledge Henry VIII as head of the Church in England, was tried and executed by being hung, drawn and quartered – one arm being suspended over Charter-house gate. He was canonized in 1970.

9 John Southworth, 1592–1654

A Roman Catholic priest, he was condemned to death under Charles I but released. While on parole he aided plague victims. He was re-arrested and executed under Cromwell, 1654. The Spanish Ambassador bought his body from the hangman, and it was eventually buried in Westminster Cathedral.

10 Henry Morse, 1595–1645

A Jesuit priest who led an eventful life, Morse was arrested five times in London, caught the plague but miraculously re-covered, and was executed at Tyburn.

TEN HAUNTED LONDON CHURCHES

1 St Peter ad Vincula, Tower Green, EC3

Britain's most haunted church is the chapel of St Peter ad Vincula within the precincts of the Tower of London. Des-cribed by Macaulay as 'the saddest spot in Christendom', it was used as the burial place for executed prisoners in the Tudor era. In 1876 Queen Victoria ordered the floor to be taken up so that the human remains beneath could be iden-tified, if possible, and given decent burial. Two hundred bodies were discovered, though few could be named. One, 'a woman of excessively delicate proportions', was thought to be Anne Boleyn. Of the many manifestations which have been reported in connection with the Chapel, the most famous occurred one night when an officer saw that the clear windows were illuminated. He climbed a ladder and saw a number of people, seemingly in fancy dress, walking in procession. It was led by a woman who reminded the amazed spectator of the paintings he had seen of Anne Boleyn. The slow parade continued for several minutes, then the figures faded and darkness returned.

2 Christ Church Greyfriars, Newgate Street, EC1

All that remains of Christ Church – formerly part of Greyfriars Monastery – is the tower, which survived the Blitz. Its ghost, which was feared down the centuries, was believed to be that of Queen Isabella, the 'She-Wolf of France', wife of Edward II, who was buried here in 1358 beside her lover, Roger Mortimer.

3 St James Garlickhythe, Garlick Hill, EC4

London's most unusual church ghost used to make rare but highly dramatic appearances in this church, which gave him his name, 'Jimmy Garlick'. Jimmy's body, dating from before the Great Fire of London, had been found in a mummified state beneath the church. Until recently it was kept as a morbid curiosity in a glass-sided coffin in the vestibule. No doubt distressed at this treatment of his mortal remains, Jimmy Garlick, a spindly figure wrapped in a shroud, sometimes materialized in the west gallery. Ten years ago the mummy was finally given a proper burial and since then the indignant phantom has been at rest.

4 St Bartholemew the Great, West Smithfield, EC1

Close to Smithfield Market, the church is haunted by the robed figure of its twelfth-century founder, Rahere, King Henry I's jester. He began the building of St Bartholemew's Church and St Bartholemew's Hospital in 1123 as an act of thanksgiving after surviving malarial fever on a pilgrimage to Rome, during which he had a vision of St Bartholemew saving him from a winged monster.

5   St Dunstan, Vyner Road, East Acton, W3

According to the psychic investigator Harry Price, St Dunstan's Church in East Acton is visited by spectral monks at four-yearly intervals. The monks wear brown habits, and many people have testified to seeing them moving in procession to the church.

6   St Giles, Camberwell High Street, SE5

St Giles has long had the reputation of being haunted by the phantom of an old priest who once served in the church – a mid-nineteenth century building on the site of a medieval structure. His apparition was last reported in 1971 walking in a churchyard passage which adjoins the church.

7   St Magnus the Martyr, Lower Thames Street, EC3

Miles Coverdale, the translator of the New Testament and vicar here from 1563–65, is believed to haunt the church of St Magnus, to which his remains were moved in 1840. (He had been buried in 1568 at St Bartholemew-by-the-Exchange, which was demolished.) Frequently those who have seen the phantom thought it was a real person and spoke to it – before it faded away in front of them.

8   St Mary, Neasden Lane, NW10

A black-robed monk has been glimpsed in the vicinity of St Mary's. The church itself, which dates from the mid-thirteenth century, is believed to be haunted, although the ghost does not actually materialize, but contents itself with rattling vestry door handles with invisible fingers.

9   St Mary the Virgin, Church Street, Twickenham

The ghost of the poet, Alexander Pope (1688–1744) began to haunt St Mary's church in 1830 when his grave was desecrated and his skull stolen for use in phrenological experiments. The figure has not been seen recently, but its limping footsteps are said still to be heard.

10 Westminster Abbey

Although Westminster Abbey has become the major British repository of the remains of sovereigns and poets, heroes and clerics, when it comes to the supernatural it can strangely offer only three rather vague spectres. One is said to be a soldier; another is believed to be John Bradshaw, the president of the court which sentenced King Charles I to death, buried in the Abbey in 1659, but later disinterred and gibbeted; and the third and best known is Father Benedictus whose rare appearances in the cloisters are always between 5 p.m. and 6 p.m. This Benedictine monk has been seen gliding several inches above the present flagging – an interesting phenomenon, since the level of the floor has become lower with the passage of time.

[List specially prepared for *The Londoner's Almanac* by Marc Alexander, author of many books on the supernatural.]

LONDON'S STRANGEST CHURCH

St Margaret Pattens, Rood Lane, Eastcheap, EC3, originally built in the 11th century and once under the patronage of Richard Whittington, was rebuilt in 1684–87 by Sir Christopher Wren after the Great Fire of London and has the only surviving example of a Wren lead-covered timber spire. It is also a treasure-trove of oddities, among which are:

1 Its name, 'Pattens', which derives from the metal and wooden clogs once worn as protection against muddy London streets. They were sold in the lane beside the church, and two pairs are exhibited in the church, together with a notice requesting women to 'leave their pattens before entering'.

2   Rare canopied pews – unique in London – for the
churchwardens. One of them bears the carved initials, 'C.W.
1686' – taken to mean Christopher Wren, although it may
simply refer to 'church warden'.

3   The copper cross, formerly on the spire, but now mounted
on the south wall, is a copy of the one on St Paul's Cathedral.

4   A beadle's pew with a so-called 'punishment bench' beneath with a carving of a devil's head. Offenders were compelled to sit there under the beadle's watchful eye and listen to
a sermon.

5   A lectern which is unusual in that the eagle grips a viper in
its talons.

6   Special rests for swords, one of which, dated 1723, has the
royal heraldic arms, those of the City, the Fishmonger's
Company and Sir Peter Delme, once Governor of the Bank of
England and Lord Mayor.

7   An hour-glass holder dating from 1750 beside the pulpit.
The hour-glass was used for timing sermons.

8   Wooden pegs on the wall of the Lady Chapel that were used
for hanging wigs during warm weather.

9   A memorial to James Donalson (d.1685) who had the
unusual job of 'City Garbler' – a person who selected spices.

10   A shrine to the crew of submarine *K4*, made of wood from
Britannia on which they trained. *K4* was sunk after its
accidental ramming on 31 January 1918.

THE TEN BEST LONDON CEMETERIES

1 Abney Park
Pride of the nonconformist cemeteries, in which many distinguished evangelical orators, theologians and missionaries lie buried.

2 Brompton
A domed chapel forms the centrepiece to an ambitious formal plan. Military burials predominate.

3 City of London
A very large cemetery with fine buildings and all in unusually good order.

4 Hampstead
Contains the graves of many famous Hampstead residents and a number of extraordinary monuments.

5 Highgate
Split into two parts, the west side is the best known of London's cemeteries, but also the least accessible. Karl Marx is buried in the east side.

6 Jewish, Willesden
Well looked after, as befits the last resting place of many well-known Jewish families, including numerous Rothschilds.

7 Kensal Green
The first 'modern' cemetery in London, founded in 1832; it also contains more fine monuments than any other.

8 Norwood
Beautifully sited on a hill, it has been terribly mutilated by bombing in the last war and by recent clearances, but the Greek enclosure survives as the most impressive burial plot in London.

9 Nunhead
One of the most devastated of the early London cemeteries, now more remarkable for its wild flora and fauna than its sepulchral origins.

10 St Marylebone
An early municipal cemetery which contains the best bronze memorials in London.

[List specially prepared for *The Londoner's Almanac* by Hugh Meller, author of *London Cemeteries* (Avebury Publishing, 1981).]

CEMETERIES IN GREATER LONDON

	Cemetery	Address	Founded	Acreage
1	Abney Park	Stoke Newington High Street, N16	1840	32
2	Acton	Park Royal Road, NW10	1895	16.5
3	Alperton	Clifford Road, Wembley	1917	10
4	Barkingside	Longwood Gardens, Ilford	E 1923 W1954	8 13.5
5	Barnes Common	Rocks Lane, SW13	1854	2
6	Battersea New	Lower Morden Lane, Morden	1891	70
7	Battersea St Mary's	Bolingbroke Grove, SW11	1860	8.5
8	Beckenham	London Road, Bromley	1877	5
9	Bexleyheath	Banks Lane, Broadway, Bexleyheath	1876	5.25
10	Brockley	Brockley Road, SE4	1858	21
11	Bromley Hill	Bromley Hill, Bromley	1905	6.25
12	Brompton	Old Brompton Road, SW5	1840	39
13	Bunhill Fields	City Road, EC1	c1665	5
14	Camberwell	Forest Hill Road, SE22	1856	29.5
15	Camberwell New	Benchley Gardens, SE23	1927	61
16	Charlton	Cemetery Lane, SE7	1855	14.5

17	Chingford Mount	Old Church Road, E4	1884	41.5
18	Chiswick Old	Corney Road, W4	1888	9
19	Chiswick New	Stavely Road, W4	1933	6.5
20	City of London	Aldersbrook Road, E12	1856	130
				[reserve 46]
21	Croydon	Mitcham Road, Croydon	1876	43
22	Crystal Palace District	Elmers End Road, SE20	1880	30
23	Ealing & Old Brentford	South Ealing Road, W5	1861	24
24	Eastcote Lane	Eastcote Lane, South Harrow	1900	3.5
25	East London	Grange Road, E13	1872	35
26	East Sheen	Sheen Road, Richmond	1903	16
27	Edmonton	Church Road, N19	1884	30
28	Edmonton & Southgate	Waterfall Road, N11	1880	11
29	Eltham	Rochester Way, SE9	1935	27.5
30	Fulham	Fulham Palace Road, SW6	1865	13
31	Golders Green Crematorium	Hoop Lane, NW11	1902	12
32	Great Northern	Brunswick Park Road, N11	1861	60
33	Greenwich	Well Hall Road, SE9	1856	22.5
34	Grove Park	Hill Lane, SE12	1935	33
35	Gunnersbury	Gunnersbury Avenue, W4	1936	22
36	Hammersmith	Margravine Road, W6	1869	17
37	Hammersmith New	Clifford Avenue, SW14	1926	26
38	Hampstead	Fortune Green Road, NW6	1876	37
39	Harrow	Pinner Road, Harrow	1887	7
40	Hendon	Holder's Hill Road, NW4	1889	40
41	Highgate	Swains Lane, N6	1839	37
42	Isleworth	Park Road, Isleworth	1879	2.5
43	Jewish	Alderney Road, E1	1697	1.25
44	Jewish	Brady Street, E1	1761	c4
45	Jewish, East Ham	Sandford Road, E6	1919	25
46	Jewish	Fulham Road, SW3	1815	c1
47	Jewish	Hoop Lane, NW11	1895	16.5
48	Jewish	Kingsbury Road, N1	1840	c.5
49	Jewish	Lauriston Road, E9	1788	2.25
50	Jewish	Montagu Road, N18	1884	c20
51	Jewish New Sephardi	Mile End Road, E1	1733	c1
52	Jewish Old Sephardi	Mile End Road, E1	1657	1.5
53	Jewish	Plashet Park, High Street, E6	1896	14
54	Jewish	Rowan Road, SW16	1915	5.5
55	Jewish West Ham	Buckingham Road, E15	1857	10.5

56	Jewish Willesden	Glebe Road, NW10	1873	23
57	Kensal Green	Harrow Road, NW10	1832	56
58	Kensington Hanwell	Broadway, W7	1855	19
59	Kingston	Bonner Hill Road, Kingston	1855	27.5
60	Lambeth	Blackshaw Road, SW17	1854	41
61	Lee	Verdant Lane, SE6	1873	65
62	Manor Park	Sebert Road, E7	1874	50
63	Merton & Sutton Joint	Garth Road, Morden	1947	57.5 [22 in use]
64	Mitcham	Church Road, Mitcham	1883	7
65	Mitcham	London Road, Mitcham	1929	18
66	Mortlake RC	North Worple Way, SW14	1852	c3
67	North Sheen	Lower Richmond Road, SW14	1926	26
68	Norwood (South Metropolitan)	Norwood High Street, SE27	1837	39
69	Nunhead	Linden Grove, SE15	1840	52
70	Old Mortlake	South Worple Way, SW14	1854	6
71	Paddington Mill Hill	Milespit Hill, NW7	1936	26
72	Paddington	Willesden Lane, NW2	1855	24
73	Pinner	Pinner Road, Pinner	1933	22.5
74	Plaistow	Burnt Ash Road, Bromley	1892	4
75	Plumstead	Wickham Lane, SE2	1890	30.5
76	Putney Lower Common	Mill Hill Road, SW13	1855	3
77	Putney Vale	Kingston Road, SW15	1891	45
78	Queens Road	Queens Road, Croydon	1861	26
79	Richmond	Grove Road, Richmond	1853	c15
80	Roding Lane North	Roding Lane North, South Woodford	1940	1.5
81	Royal Hospital, Chelsea Burial Ground	Royal Hospital Road, SW3	1692	1
82	Royal Hospital, Greenwich	Chevening Road, SE10	1857	6
83	St Marylebone	East End Road, N3	1854	33
84	St Mary's RC	Harrow Road, NW10	1858	29
85	St Pancras & Islington	High Road, N2	1854	182
86	St Patrick's RC	Langthorne Road, E11	1868	43
87	St Thomas's RC	Rylston Road, SW6	1849	c.5
88	Streatham	Garratt Lane, SW17	1892	36
89	Streatham Park	Rowan Road, SW16	1909	70
90	Sutton	Alcorn Close, Sutton	1889	19.5

91	Teddington	Shacklegate Lane, Teddington	1879	9
92	Tottenham	Prospect Place, N17	1856	56
93	Tottenham Park	Montagu Road, N18	1912	c6
94	Tower Hamlets	Southern Grove, E3	1841	33
95	Twickenham	Hospital Bridge Road, Twickenham	1868	20
96	Walthamstow	Queen's Road, E17	1872	11
97	Wandsworth	Magdalen Road, SW18	1878	34
98	West Ham	Cemetery Road, E7	1857	20
99	Westminster	Uxbridge Road, W7	1854	23
100	Willesden	Franklyn Road, NW10	1891	26
101	Wimbledon	Gap Road, SW19	1896	28
102	Woodgrange Park	Romford Road, E7	1890	28
103	Woolwich	Kings Highway/Camdale Road, SE18	1856	32.5

[Based on Hugh Meller's *London Cemeteries* (Avebury Publishing, 1981).]

REIGNING MONARCHS BURIED IN LONDON

Monarch	Died	Buried
Boadicea	c60–61AD	Reputedly beneath Platform 10, King's Cross Station
Ethelred II	1016	Old St Paul's Cathedral (destroyed)
Edward the Confessor	1066	Westminster Abbey
Henry III	1272	Westminster Abbey
Edward I	1307	Westminster Abbey
Edward III	1377	Westminster Abbey
Richard II	1400	Westminster Abbey
Henry V	1422	Westminster Abbey
Edward V ('Prince in the Tower')	1483?	Westminster Abbey*

Henry VII	1509	Westminster Abbey
Edward VI	1553	Westminster Abbey
Jane (Lady Jane Grey)	1554	Tower of London
Mary I	1558	Westminster Abbey
Elizabeth I	1603	Westminster Abbey
James I	1625	Westminster Abbey
Charles II	1685	Westminster Abbey
Mary II	1694	Westminster Abbey
William III	1702	Westminster Abbey
Anne	1714	Westminster Abbey
George II	1760	Westminster Abbey

* Bones found in the Tower of London, supposedly those of Edward V, were buried in 1678.

TEN UNUSUAL LONDON EPITAPHS

Exit Burbage
[Richard Burbage, died 1619]
(St Leonard, Shoreditch, E1)

Shee first deceased, Hee for a little Tryd
To live without her, lik'd it not and dyd.
[Margaret & John Whiting, died 1680 and 1681]
(St Bartholemew-the-Great, West Smithfield, EC1)

Here lyeth wrapt in Clay
The Body of William Wray
I have no more to say.
(St Michael, Crooked Lane – demolished 1831)

Here lies Dame Mary Page, relict of Sir Gregory Page, Bart.
She departed this life March 4th, 1728, in the 56th year of her
age. In 67 months she was tap'd 66 times. Had taken away
240 gallons of water, without ever repining at her case, or
ever fearing the operation.
(Bunhill Fields, City Road, EC1)

This tomb was erected by William Picket, of the City of
London, goldsmith, on the melancholy death of his daughter,
Elizabeth. A testimony of respect from greatly afflicted
parents.
In memory of Elizabeth Picket, spinster, who died December
11, 1781. Aged 23 Years. This much lamented young person
expired in consequence of her clothes taking fire the
preceding evening. Reader – if ever you should witness such
an affecting scene; recollect that the only method to
extinguish the flame is to stifle it by an immediate
covering.
(St Mary's Old Church, Stoke Newington, N16)

Remember the Sabbath Day
To Keep it Holy
To the Memory of
Alexander MacGeorge aged 11 years
William MacGeorge aged 9 years
George Smith aged 12 years
Robert Johnston aged 12 years
Alexander Jones aged 12 years
Who were drowned while amusing themselves on the ice on
Bowater pond on Sunday the 6th day of February 1831 and
are interred in this grave.
The Jurors who were present at the Coroner's Court on the
melancholy occasion have caused this memorial to be erected
by public subscriptions to commemorate the mournful event
and more especially to impress upon the young the necessity
and importance of remembering their Creator in the days of
their youth and excite them to avoid the sin and danger of
violating the Sabbath Day.
(St Mary Magdalene, Woolwich, SE18)

Sacred to the memory of
Major James Brush
who was killed by the accidental discharge of a pistol by
his orderly
14th April 1831
Well done, good and faithful servant.
(St Mary Magdalene, Woolwich, SE18)

Sacred to the memory of
Edward Hunt
late of Islington
who died a martyr to the Gout
August 18th, 1848, aged 53 years.
(Highgate Cemetery, N6)

Sacred to the memory of
Edward Fitzgibbon Esq
who died the 19th of November, 1857, aged 54.
Author of numerous works on angling and was better known
as Ephemera. This monument is erected by a few of his
friends in admiration of his piscatory writings.
(Highgate Cemetery, N6)

I was not and was conceived.
I loved, and did a little work.
I am not, and grieve not.
[Professor W. K. Clifford, died 1879]
(Highgate Cemetery, N6)

SEVEN UNUSUAL DEATHS IN LONDON

1 Francis Bacon

The First Baron Verulam and Viscount St Albans, the noted
philosopher, writer and statesman, died at Highgate on 9 April

1626 as a result of a severe cold caught the previous month while he was stuffing a chicken with snow in an early experiment in the production of frozen food.

2 Thomas Otway

In 1685 in the traditional style of many writers, the 33-year-old dramatist Thomas Otway was starving to death in a garret when a friend kindly gave him some bread. The first mouthful choked him to death. He was buried at St Clement Danes in the Strand.

3 Franz Kotzwara

In 1793 Susanna Hill, a prostitute in Covent Garden, was tried for the murder of Polish-born composer Franz Kotzwara. He had persuaded her to hang him as part of a bizarre sex ritual, but had given her instructions to cut him down and revive him – which she unfortunately failed to do. She was acquitted.

4 John Charles Brook

During the first royal command performance at the Haymarket Theatre in 1794 a riot broke out and 15 people were crushed to death. Three years later, also in the presence of the Royal Family, John Charles Brook, a member of the College of Heralds, was killed when part of the ceiling fell on him. There is a memorial tablet to him at St Benet Paul's Wharf.

5 Thomas Beale

Thomas Beale's grave at St Mary's, Battersea, records the cause of his death on 12 February 1816 as 'Burnt to death on a lime kiln at Nine Elms'.

6 Chung Ling-Soo

The 'Chinese Magician', Chung Ling-Soo (the stage name of an American, William Ellisworth Robinson) was fatally wounded on 23 March 1918 at the Wood Green Empire Theatre when his most famous trick, in which he appeared to catch bullets in his teeth, went disastrously wrong and he was shot in the chest.

7 Keith Relf

On 14 May 1976, Keith Relf, the lead singer of the successful rock band, The Yardbirds, was electrocuted by his own guitar.

THE TEN WORST YEARS TO HAVE LIVED IN LONDON

1 1348–49

The Black Death struck in November; by May of the next year, a total estimated at between 50000 and 100000 people (although this appears to exaggerate the probable population of London at the time) were dead.

2 1381

The Peasants' Revolt, led by Wat Tyler, descended on London. Tyler was killed and the quelling of the Revolt led to many executions.

3 1664–65

The Great Plague wiped out a large proportion of London's population, variously estimated at between 10000 and 100000.

4 1666

The Great Fire of London started on 2 September. Most of the City – almost 400 acres, containing about 13200 houses and 87 churches – was destroyed.

5 1683–84

One of the severest frosts of all time lasted from November until the following April. The Thames was iced over from early December until 4 February and a massive 'Frost Fair' held on it.

6 1780

The Gordon Riots broke out on 2 June. Although nominally anti-Catholic, they turned into a general riot in which numerous buildings were looted or burned down. At least 565 and perhaps as many as 850 people were killed – the largest number in any riot in Britain. The 21 ringleaders were hanged.

7 1858

Known as the year of the 'Great Stink', when sewage draining into the Thames, combined with a hot summer, made the river unapproachable. Cholera epidemics were common – as many as 12 847 Londoners died in the last three months of 1849 – and the 'Great Stink' was the final spur to the major improvement of London's sewers in the 1860s.

8 1918

During the final months of the First World War, Great Britain was hit by an influenza epidemic in which 225 000 died – many of them in London.

9 1940–41

September 1940 to May 1941 was the worst period of the blitz, when an estimated 18 800 tons of bombs rained down on London. Some 1436 people were killed on the night of 10–11 May 1941 alone, and even people sheltering in tube stations previously believed to be safe were killed when Marble Arch, Balham and Bank received direct hits.

10 1952

One of the worst of the great London fogs of modern times occurred in December and was said to have caused the deaths of about 4000 Londoners. Smoke controls in recent years have virtually ended the centuries-old reputation of 'a foggy day in London town'.

AIR RAIDS ON LONDON

Between 1939 and 1945, 3.5 million houses were bombed, and over 15000 people were killed in the blitz on London.

Number of air raid warnings

1939	3
1940	417
1941	154
1942	25
1943	95
1944	508
1945	22
Total:	1224

BOOKS DESTROYED IN AIR RAIDS

Vast numbers of books were destroyed during the blitz. Among the major losses were:

Newspaper Library, Colindale
Some 30000 bound volumes of newspapers, many irreplaceable, were destroyed on 20 October 1940.

University College, Gower Street
In October 1940 70000 books were consumed in a fire started by an incendiary bomb.

Simpkin Marshall & Co.
Simpkin Marshall were the largest book distributors in the world, with huge warehouses in Ave Maria Lane, Stationers' Hall Court, Amen Corner, Paternoster Row and Ludgate Hill. When they were destroyed by incendiary bombing on 29

December 1940, about 4 000 000 books were lost. Many publishers in the area also lost their stock during the same raid – perhaps a further 2 000 000 books.

The Guildhall
About 25 000 books, mainly relating to the history of London, were destroyed by bombing on 29 December 1940.

National Central Library, Malet Place
On 17 April 1941 110 000 books were lost.

The British Museum
A raid on the night of 10–11 May 1941 destroyed 150 000 books. To this day, readers are liable to have their book applications returned marked, 'destroyed by bombing'.

Lambeth Palace
On 10 May 1941 about 150 bookshelves were destroyed and 8000 books severely damaged by a fire caused by bombing, although some were salvaged.

Inner Temple Library
About 45 000 books were destroyed in May 1941.

Gray's Inn
The library was gutted and 32 000 books, including some rare legal works and bibles, destroyed in May 1941.

London Library
Around 16 000 books were destroyed on 23 February 1944.

TEN FIRES OF LONDON

The Great Fire of 1666 is well known. It broke out on 2 September, destroying over 400 acres, principally in the City, including 87 churches. But London has also experienced many other major fires, among which are:

1 St Paul's Cathedral, 961 etc
St Paul's was burnt down in 961 and its replacement in 1087. The Norman cathedral, much larger than the present one, was damaged by lightning and fire on several occasions, and eventually totally destroyed in the Great Fire.

2 Southwark, 1676
Ten years after the Great Fire, on 26 May Southwark had its own Great Fire in which the Town Hall and 624 houses were destroyed.

3 Custom House, 1814
A large fire on 12 February destroyed a huge collection of valuable paintings and books.

4 Palace of Westminster, 1834
During the burning of a vast collection of wooden sticks once used as tallies by the Court of Exchequer, the House of Lords was set on fire and destroyed, along with the House of Commons and most of the rest of the Palace of Westminster.

5 Lloyds Coffee House and Royal Exchange, 1838
Both were destroyed on 10 January by a fire believed to have started in Lloyds.

6 Tower of London, 1841
The armoury containing about 280 000 weapons was destroyed on 30 October.

7 Tooley Street, 1861
On 22 June a huge fire destroyed buildings in Tooley Street resulting in £2 million-worth of damage. James Braidwood,

Chief of the Metropolitan Fire Brigade, was killed by a falling wall. There is a memorial to him by S. H. Gardner, erected in 1862.

8 Alexandra Palace, 1873
Alexandra Palace, North London's rival to the Crystal Palace, was completely destroyed on 9 June – just two weeks after it opened. It was rebuilt and, after a century of mixed fortunes, burned down again in 1980.

9 The Pantechnicon, 1874
This large warehouse complex in Motcomb Street caught fire on 13 February, destroying £2 million-worth of goods stored there. Its original frontage withstood the blaze and can still be seen.

10 Crystal Palace, 1936
Originally constructed for the 1851 Great Exhibition in Hyde Park, the building was dismantled and re-erected at Sydenham in 1854 where it was used as an entertainment centre. It caught fire on 30 November and was completely destroyed.

LONDON FIRE BRIGADE [1983]

Total no. of calls	117253
Total no. of fires	50176
Fire brigade personnel killed	0
Adult lives lost	141
Child lives lost	22
Fire brigade personnel injured	103
Adult injuries	1044
Child injuries	9
Total no. of rescues	975
Personnel	<7000

Number of fire stations	114
Total cost of service	£139254000
Oldest fire station:	Clerkenwell, built 1870
	at a cost of £3968

FIVE FAMOUS LONDON SIEGES

1 Sidney Street, E1

On 3 January 1911 the police believed they had tracked down two members of a gang of foreign anarchists, one of whom was thought to be the notorious 'Peter the Painter', to 100 Sidney Street. A policeman who knocked on the door was shot; 400 further armed police, members of the Scots Guards, Royal Engineers and the Fire Brigade – as well as Winston Churchill who was then Home Secretary – promptly descended on the house and the Siege of Sidney Street began. It did not last long: at 1 p.m. the house caught fire and the two men died in the blaze. Neither of the bodies was that of Peter the Painter. He was never heard of again, and the circumstances of the Siege were never fully explained.

2 Spaghetti House, SW1

On 28 September 1975, members of the Black Liberation Front held up seven Italian members of staff of the restaurant at 77 Knightsbridge after a bungled attempt to seize their takings. Among their demands was one to release two prisoners who the police announced were not in fact in custody. The hostages became friendly with their captors and the gunmen surrendered five days later without harming them.

3 Balcombe Street, NW1

From 7 to 13 December 1975 four IRA gunmen took refuge in No. 22B Balcombe Street after a police chase. They held an elderly couple hostage, but the siege eventually ended without injury when the gunmen surrendered.

4   Iranian Embassy, SW7

The Embassy at 27 Princes Gate became the first political siege to be televised live when it was held between 30 April and 5 May 1980 by Iranian gunmen demanding autonomy for Khuzestan and the release of prisoners in Iran. It ended dramatically when the SAS stormed the building killing five of the gunmen and releasing the nineteen hostages unharmed.

5   St James's Square, SW1

The Libyan People's Bureau at 5 St James's Square was besieged when on 17 April 1984 gunmen within the building fired on demonstrators outside, killing Policewoman Yvonne Fletcher. Diplomatic immunity made it impossible for the police to enter the building or to arrest the suspects and when the siege ended ten days later they were deported – presumably with their murder weapon. A memorial to Yvonne Fletcher commemorates this disgraceful affair.

TEN LONDON EXPLOSIONS

The Gunpowder Plot of 1605 was London's most famous explosion that never happened; here are ten that did:

1   All Hallows, Barking, 1649

On 4 January 27 barrels of gunpowder exploded next to the church. About 50 houses were destroyed, including the Rose Tavern where a parish dinner was in progress, killing many people.

2   Belvedere Powder Magazine explosion, 1864

About 104000 lbs of gunpowder exploded at the Plumstead factory of Hall & Co. on 1 October, killing 13. It is said that the explosion was heard 50 miles away.

3 Clerkenwell Prison, 1867

On 13 December during a bungled attempt to release the Fenian prisoners Burke and Casey, the prison wall was destroyed – along with the houses opposite. Six people were killed outright, at least six died later and 120 were injured.

4 Regent's Park explosion, 1874

At dawn on 10 October a barge, *Tilbury*, loaded with petroleum and 5 tons of gunpowder caught fire and exploded as it passed under a bridge – now known as Macclesfield Bridge, or, popularly, 'Blow Up Bridge' – on the Regent's Canal. The crew of four were blown to pieces – as were many neighbouring houses, including that of the painter, Lawrence Alma-Tadema – and animals escaped from the nearby Zoo.

5 'Dynamiters' Outrage', 1883

On 30 October 1883 a bomb planted by the so-called 'Dynamiters' (Irish revolutionaries) exploded on the Metropolitan Railway near Praed Street, shattering two third-class carriages and injuring 62 people.

6 Victoria Station, 1884

A bomb left in the cloakroom of Victoria Station on 27 February destroyed the building and injured two people.

7 House of Commons, Westminster Hall and Tower of London, 1885

On 24 January a bomb exploded, injuring two policemen on duty in the House of Commons. One of them, William Cole, was awarded the Albert Medal for bravery, having carried another blazing parcel from the building. On the same day bombs went off causing further injury and damage at Westminster Hall and the Tower of London. In 1885 the men responsible, Irish extremists John Gilbert Cunningham and Harry Burton, were convicted and sentenced to life imprisonment.

8 Silvertown, 1917

The scene of the dreadful explosion at the Brunner Mond Chemical Works, E16. Some 50 tons of TNT blew up in a fire killing 69 and injuring over 300, with over £2 million worth of damage.

9 Harrods bombing, 1983

On 17 December an IRA car bomb killed six – three of them police officers – and severely injured many others during a busy Saturday when Harrods was full of Christmas shoppers.

10 Putney gas explosion, 1985

On 10 January 1985, a gas explosion destroyed the centre section of a three-storey block of flats, Newnham House, Putney Hill, killing eight people and injuring seven.

TEN COMMONEST CASUALTY COMPLAINTS IN LONDON HOSPITALS

1 Cuts
2 Bruises
3 Dog bites
4 Sprained ankles
5 Eye injuries
6 Nose bleeds
7 Minor burns
8 Toothache
9 Head injuries
10 Fractures – especially wrists in winter

EIGHT LONDON SUICIDES

1 Thomas Chatterton
The seventeen-year-old poet drank arsenic at 39 Brooke Street, EC1, on 24 August 1770.

2 Robert Clive
Robert Clive – 'Clive of India' – died at his house at 45 Berkeley Square, after taking an overdose of laudanum, on 22 November 1774.

3 John Williams
The chief suspect in the Ratcliffe Highway Murder case [see also *Eight Famous London Murder Cases*, p. 187], Williams committed suicide by hanging himself. He was buried on 30 December 1811 according to custom – at a crossroads (New Road and Cannon Street Road) with a stake through his body – probably the last occasion this was carried out in London.

4 Robert Castlereagh
On 12 August 1822 Castlereagh, the Foreign Secretary, cut his throat with a penknife at his Foots Cray house.

5 Benjamin Haydon
Although a talented painter, Haydon upset many of his clients by failing to fulfil commissions. The public ignored his exhibition at the Egyptian Hall, Piccadilly in favour of a rival exhibition – that of the midget, Tom Thumb. In a fit of depression, Haydon failed again – this time, to shoot himself – but he finally succeeded in cutting his throat with a razor, and died on 22 June 1846.

6 A. Smart
Smart, a watchmaker, made an extravagantly public exit by hurling himself off the whispering gallery at St Paul's Cathedral on 14 March 1856.

7 Thomas Lee

Lee leaped to his death off the North Tower of Crystal Palace on 18 February 1868.

8 John William Godward

Godward was a painter who produced poor imitations of the Roman scenes that made Sir Lawrence Alma-Tadema famous. In 1922 he contrived to burn his head off over a gas stove.

EIGHT FAMOUS LONDON MURDER CASES

1 The Princes in the Tower

Edward V and his brother the Duke of York were, allegedly, murdered in the Tower of London in about 1483 by two hired assassins, Miles Forest and John Dighton, acting for the Princes' uncle, Richard III. Two skeletons were found in 1674 and in 1678 reinterred in Westminster Abbey. Various historians – and particularly the Richard III Society – have endeavoured to absolve Richard from blame. In 1933 the urn containing their remains was examined with little new evidence coming to light, and the verdict must remain 'not proven'.

2 Christopher Marlowe

The great English dramatist (1564–1593), the author of *The Tragedy of Doctor Faustus* and numerous other works, met his end in a Deptford tavern on 20 May 1593. An enquiry held at the time suggested that it was a result of a fight with his drinking companion, Ingram Frisar, who stabbed him with a dagger, but evidence points to the fact that Marlowe was a spy and there may well have been a deeper motive. He is commemorated on a plaque on the wall of St Nicholas, Deptford Green, SE8, where he was buried.

3 The Ratcliffe Highway murders

Two incidents in which seven people were butchered took place in neighbouring buildings in this Thameside area in December 1811. On the 7th Mr Marr, a shopkeeper, and his wife, child and assistant died; then on the 11th the landlord of the King's Arms, Mr Williamson, his wife and a servant were found dead with terrible wounds. A man called John Williams was arrested but hanged himself on 15 December, before he could be brought to trial.

4 Spencer Perceval

Spencer Perceval (1762–1812) has the doubtful distinction of being Britain's only Prime Minister to have been murdered. As he entered the House of Commons on 11 May 1812, a bankrupt Liverpool broker, John Bellingham, shot him dead. Bellingham was swiftly tried and hanged a week later.

5 Jack the Ripper

Perhaps London's most famous murderer – if the five murders were all committed by one man. All the victims were East End prostitutes, viciously attacked and mutilated in the Whitechapel area between August and November 1888. No one was ever brought to justice, but speculation as to the identity of the 'Ripper' has continued for nearly a century – the range of suspects includes a deranged freemason and the Duke of Clarence.

6 Dr Crippen

Dr Hawley Harvey Crippen poisoned his wife with an overdose of hyoscine, at their house in Hilldrop Crescent, Holloway (Margaret Bondfield House now stands on the site). He dismembered her body and buried parts in his cellar, then fled for Canada with his mistress, Ethel Le Neve, who was disguised as a boy. While at sea, his crime was discovered, the ship telegraphed and Crippen arrested in Quebec. He thus then became the first murderer caught by radio. He was tried at the Central Criminal Court in 1910 and hanged.

7 The Brighton trunk murder

A naked female torso was discovered at Brighton Station on 17 June 1934, minus its legs which were later found at King's Cross Station. Neither the identity of the girl nor her murderer have ever been established.

8 Dennis Nilsen

Arrested on 9 February 1983, Nilsen admitted to at least fifteen murders during the previous four years at his house at 23 Cranley Gardens, N10. His crimes were revealed when workmen were called in to unblock drains that were found to be clogged with human remains. He was sentenced to life imprisonment.

[For a ninth London murder case, see '10 Rillington Place', under *Ten Famous London Addresses*, p. 100.]

TEN ODD LONDON LAWS

1 The City of Westminster (Section 15 of the Open Spaces Act, 1906, subsection 21.i) prohibits anyone from beating a carpet in a park.

2 Under Section 23 of the Royal and Other Parks and Gardens Regulations of 1977, 'touching a Pelican' is forbidden – unless written permission is first obtained.

3 Uniformed beadles are on hand in Burlington Arcade to prevent anyone from whistling or opening an umbrella in the Arcade.

4 On Wimbledon Common, 'every person playing golf is required to wear a red outer garment'.

5 Signs on Albert Bridge demand that troops break step before marching over it, for fear that the vibration might cause its collapse.

6 The Silver Cross public house, 33 Whitehall, SW1, was licensed as a brothel by Charles I. Despite – or perhaps because of – its proximity to the Houses of Parliament; as far as anyone can tell, this licence has never been revoked.

7 The Mayflower, 117 Rotherhithe Street, SE16, is Britain's only pub licensed to sell British *and* American postage stamps.

8 The Castle, 34 Cowcross Street, EC1, is the only public house in England with a pawnbroker's licence.

9 The owner or driver of a London taxi 'may refuse to convey a person suffering from a notifiable disease [smallpox, cholera, plague, typhus, etc] until paid a sum sufficient to cover loss and expense incurred in having the vehicle disinfected'.

10 Only the sovereign, and the Dyers and Vintners companies are allowed to own swans on the Thames. Their beaks are marked at the annual 'Swan Upping' so that they can be identified.

SOME METROPOLITAN POLICE FACTS AND FIGURES [1983]

Number of police officers	26 806
Mounted police officers	210
Police horses	176
Notifiable offences	659 293
of which:	
Violence against the person	17 820
Sexual offences	2 837
Robbery	12 037
Burglary and 'going equipped'	153 620
Theft and handling stolen goods	353 078
Fraud and forgery	29 714
Criminal damage	87 873
Other	2 314

Theft of pedal cycle	22438
Arson	3598
Drug trafficking	1499
Blackmail	180
Kidnapping	59
Bigamy	25

| Robberies in which firearms carried | 1333 |

| Missing persons (includes 416 boys and 278 girls under 14) | 7692 |

Burglar alarm calls received	196190
False alarms	193470
Genuine calls	2720

| Bodies recovered from the Thames | 58 |

London Weekend Television's 'Police 5' programme success rate: 232 cases shown; 51 arrests directly attributed to appeals.

TEN UNUSUAL ITEMS LEFT ON LONDON TUBES AND BUSES

False teeth
An outboard motor
A television
A stuffed gorilla
A three-foot long spanner
A box of glass eyes
A bed
An artificial hand
A bag of human bones
A five-foot garden seat

Lost Property Statistics: London Tubes and Buses

In 1983, 130 460 items were found on London tubes and buses including:

22 735 umbrellas
24 943 handbags, purses, etc
17 864 items of clothing
14 034 books
 9 398 pairs of gloves
 8 572 cases and bags
 1 630 odd gloves

London Bus Statistics

Length of route run over	163 458 000 miles
Buses: single deck	568
Buses: double deck	5070
Fuel consumption per annum	22 845 857 gallons
Passengers carried per annum	1 088 million
Passengers carried per weekday	3 390 000
Passenger miles per annum	2 442 million
Average distance travelled	2.2 miles
Average fare per journey	24.4p
Average fare per passenger mile	10.8p
Average speed	11.3 mph
Number of bus stops	17 000
Number of bus shelters	8 600
Longest route	21.10 miles, N97 – Liverpool Street to Heathrow Central

Shortest route	1.3 miles, 248A – Upminster (Corbets Tey) to Upminster Station
Route using most buses	12, Norwood Junction to Harlesden – 58 during peak
Most frequent service	253, Aldgate to Warren Street (Cambridge Heath to Holloway section) – 24 per hour during peak
Point served by most buses	Trafalgar Square, 450 per hour during peak
Number of bus garages	61
Largest garage	Holloway, 146 buses
Smallest garage	Loughton, 37 buses

Ticket machines

Type	Number in service	Paper rolls consumed per year
Gibson	4558	1574400
Almex 'E'	5621	732800

Staff employed

Drivers and conductors	18800
Garage engineering	4000
Works engineering	2500
Traffic staff	2400
Administration and training	1800
Total	**29500**

[1983/84 figures]

LONDON UNDERGROUND STATISTICS

Length of route run over	247 miles
Rolling stock: motor	2457
Rolling stock: trailer	1418
Passengers carried per annum	563 million*
Passengers carried per weekday	1844000*
Passenger miles per annum	2703 million*
Average distance travelled	4.8 miles*
Average fare per journey	50.7p
Average fare per passenger mile	10.6p
Average speed	20.5 mph
Number of stations served	272

Six busiest stations

Station	Passengers per year
Victoria	48 million
Oxford Circus	39 million
King's Cross	32 million
Liverpool Street	30 million
Waterloo	25 million
Piccadilly Circus	21 million

Longest escalator	Leicester Square, 161.5 ft
Shortest escalator	Chancery Lane, 30 ft
Deepest lift shaft	Hampstead, 181 ft
Shortest lift shaft	Chalk Farm, 30.5 ft
Fastest lift	Hampstead, 800 ft per minute
Stations with most platforms	Moorgate and Baker Street – both 10

Deepest tunnel	221 ft below ground level (Northern Line, Holly Bush Hill, Hampstead)
Deepest station	Hampstead, 192 ft below ground level
Highest line	Metropolitan Line, beyond Amersham Station, c500 ft above sea level
Highest station	Amersham, c490 ft above sea level

Staff employed

Engineering	12 200
Traffic control	7 100
Train drivers and guards	4 000
Police	300
Administration	300
Total	**23 900**

Station with largest car park	Wembley Park, 634 car spaces

* Includes journeys originating on British Rail [1983/84 figures]

LONDON'S AIRPORTS: FACTS AND FIGURES

HEATHROW

Aviation in the area now occupied by Heathrow dates from Richard Fairey's Great West Aerodrome, opened in 1929 and used principally for test flights. During the Second World War, an airport was needed to handle large aircraft, and the area north-east of Stanwell was selected as the most appropriate site. Work on a military airfield at Heathrow (the ancient village of this name was on the present site of Terminal 3) started in 1944, but the War was over before it was completed and it was re-planned as a civil airport. The first flight from the new airport (a British South American Lancastrian) took off on 1 January 1946 and Heathrow was officially opened on 31 May of the same year. It has grown steadily and is now the busiest international airport in the world, handling two-thirds of all UK airline arrivals.

The terminals

Terminal 1 (opened 1968) handles 10.7 million passengers each year

Terminal 2 (opened 1955) handles over 6 million passengers each year

Terminal 3 (opened 1962) handles 10 million passengers each year

Terminal 4 (costing £200 million and opening in October 1985) will handle 8 million passengers a year, enabling Heathrow to handle a total of 38 million passengers a year in the future.

Passenger traffic growth	
1950	523351
1960	5380937
1970	15606719
1980	27770643

* Between 1981 and 1983, as a result of the economic recession, the total number of passengers declined, but in 1984 there was an upturn, and the total was similar to 1980.

* Heathrow handles some 16% by value of Britain's trade – about £16.6 billion in 1983 – making it also Britain's leading port.

* Over 70 different airlines fly from Heathrow to over 200 direct destinations.

* Heathrow's total income in 1983/84 was £204 446 000, and expenditure was £154 139 000.

* The largest number of aircraft movements in a single day was 986 on 19 July 1974. The total in 1983/84 was 286 609.

* The largest number of passengers handled in a single day was 112 880 on Sunday 31 August 1980. On the same day, Heathrow recorded its largest-ever hourly passenger flow of 10 500. The average is 73 000 a day. Passengers use 4500 baggage trolleys – the largest collection in the world – are met by over 30 000 non-flying visitors and consume 16 500 cups of tea and coffee, over 4000 pints of beer, and 2800 sandwiches a day.

* Every year Heathrow's duty-free shops sell 500 million cigarettes, 4 million bottles of liquor (1 million gallons), 16 million cigars, 40 tons of pipe tobacco and 1 million bottles of perfume.

* Heathrow's busiest traffic route is that linking it with Paris, Charles de Gaulle, in 1983/84 amounting to 1 891 000 passengers, or 7% of the total. New York, JFK, comes second at 948 000 (3.5%).

* Heathrow covers an area of 2958 acres (1197 hectares). The perimeter road is over 9.5 miles long. The longest runway (28R/10L) is 3902 m (12 800 ft or 2.42 miles) long.

* The road tunnel leading to the Central Terminal Area is 2080 ft long and 86 ft wide. It has a capacity of 3000 vehicles per hour in each direction. Over 12 million vehicles pass through it every year.

* There are 125 aircraft stands in the central area, with a further 26 in the cargo area.

* The total number of employees in 1983/84 was 44312 (30644 airline staff, 7189 working for concessionaires, 3545 British Airports Authority staff, 2543 government officials, excluding police, and 371 contractors' employees).

* Heathrow is increasingly popular – or, at least, less unpopular: the number of written complaints in the financial year 1983/84 amounted to 2714 (less than one per 10000 passengers). In 1981/82 there were 4281. Of the 1983/84 total, 15% related to catering, 12% to baggage, 33% to 'other facilities' and 40% were non-specific.

GATWICK

* Gatwick is, perhaps surprisingly, the fourth busiest airport in the world (after Heathrow, New York JFK and Frankfurt).

* London's second airport handled 12.7 million passengers in 1983/84 – double the number handled in 1976/77. The largest number handled in a single day was 74000 on 31 July 1983.

* A total of 13050 people were employed in 1983/84.

STANSTED

Stansted may become 'London's Third Airport' in the 1990s.

* In 1983/84 Stansted handled 357000 passengers – a 19.6% increase over the previous year, making it Britain's fastest-growing airport.

* A total of 1453 people were employed in 1983/84.

London Postal Region Statistics

Number of postboxes	12512
Sorting offices	175
Main post offices	367
Sub post offices	1405
Vehicles	5145
Annual mileage	43000000
Annual fuel consumption (galls.)	2200000
Delivery points (Inner Area)	1706000
Delivery points (Outer Area)	1697000
Letters handled per week	73100000
Parcels handled per week	2000000

Staff

Postmen/women and drivers	23978
Sorters	6994
Counter clerks	5304
Administrative	4367
Engineers	2225
Cleaners and other grades	2806
Total staff	45674

London Letter Boxes

The first roadside letter boxes were introduced in the Channel Islands in 1852, following a successful pilot study set up by Anthony Trollope, then a surveyor's clerk for the Western Postal Division of England. One of these early boxes remains in use in St Peter Port, Guernsey. Boxes appeared on the mainland the following year.

The first London pillar boxes were installed by Rowland Hill, the Secretary to the Post Office, in 1855. These were rectangular boxes with a large ball on top and situated in Fleet Street, Strand, Pall Mall, Piccadilly and Rutland Gate. None of them has survived. The oldest boxes still in use in London are the cast-iron 'Penfold' boxes of 1872, designed by an architect, J. W. Penfold and manufactured by Cochrane & Co of Dudley. Twenty-nine of these remain in use in the London postal area. They are hexagonal with an ornamental canopy decorated with acanthus leaves and topped with an acanthus bud with a row of balls along each edge. Originally painted in sage green, they have been the familiar 'pillar box red' since 1874. New boxes introduced in 1879 were cylindrical, and this has been the shape used ever since (apart from a brief trial of a square box in the 1960s). They came in two sizes – the smaller 'B' box weighing around 7 cwt and the larger 'A' box about 10 cwt. They extend for some 21 inches below the ground. The oval 'C' type box with two apertures for 'Town' and 'Country' was introduced in the 1890s and weighs one ton. During the 1960s most of the older boxes were removed from Central London and replaced by boxes with two apertures, bearing the Elizabeth II cipher.

TEN OF THE OLDEST (PENFOLD) LETTER BOXES IN LONDON

NW3	Hampstead High Street (near Hampstead underground station)
NW8	Prince Albert Road (near London Zoo)
W2	Kensington Palace Gardens
W8	Kensington High Street (near Commonwealth Institute)
W8	Pembroke Gardens
W10	Oxford Gardens
W10	Telford Road
SW3	St Leonard's Terrace
SW4	The Chase
SW19	Woodhayes Road (opposite 'The Crooked Billet')

TEN EXAMPLES OF LETTER BOX TYPES IN LONDON

Victoria	Penfold hexagonal box, 1872 (e.g.: Wellington Place, NW8, near Lord's)
Victoria	Double aperture box, 1899 (e.g.: Finsbury Pavement, EC2, near Moorgate underground station)
Victoria	Free-standing wall box, 1881 (e.g.: St Cross Street, EC1)
Victoria	Wall box of 1873–79 made by Eagle Range (e.g.: Hampstead High Street, NW3)
Edward VII	Double aperture box with VR door (Unique – south end of Gray's Inn Road, WC1)
Edward VII	Free-standing wall box with ball on top (Unique – Waterloo Station)
Edward VII	Free-standing wall boxes (e.g.: Great Russell Street, WC1, outside British Museum)
Edward VIII	Only 'A' and 'B' size pillar boxes made, 1936 (e.g.: Elliot Road, NW4, near Brent Cross Shopping Centre)
Elizabeth II	Square boxes made by Vandyke, 1968 (e.g.: St Paul's Cathedral precinct)
Elizabeth II	'K' type box, introduced in 1980 (e.g.: Prince Consort Road, SW7, near Royal Albert Hall)

[Information and lists specially prepared for *The Londoner's Almanac* by Dr David Rubra of The Letter Box Study Group. Further information about the Group may be obtained from their Publications Officer, Mr I. G. Wilkinson, 17 Germains Close, Chesham, Bucks., HP5 1JJ.]

LONDON TELEPHONE STATISTICS

Number of telephones

Public	10 765
Private: main	2.6 million
Private: extensions	3.1 million
Business: main	0.9 million
Business: extensions	2.9 million

Number of households with a telephone: 86 per 100
UK average: 75 per 100
Number of calls per annum: 4 113 300 000
Number of international calls per annum: 119 800 000
Number of calls to Timeline (formerly 'Speaking Clock'):
82 800 000
Number of telephone directory entries (including community and Telex directories): 8 500 000

LONDON TELEPHONE EXCHANGES

Before 1927 telephone calls had to be connected by the operator. The first automatic telephone exchange, permitting the user to dial the required number direct, was opened in Holborn on 12 November 1927 and was soon followed by others covering the entire London area. The naming of these exchanges presented enormous problems. The number/letter equivalents available on the dial were:

1		6	MN
2	ABC	7	PRS
3	DEF	8	TUV
4	GHI	9	WXY
5	JKL	0	O

A number might thus be dialled as 'HOLborn 1234', giving the numerical equivalent '405 1234'. But clearly, certain local names had identical letters – such as Hampstead and Hammersmith, Stratford and Streatham, Chiswick and Chingford – while others had the same numerical equivalents – such as Acton and Battersea. Because of this many names could not be used and alternatives were sought. Criteria in finding suitable names were that they should have unique three-letter and numerical equivalent prefixes, should be easily remembered, not confusable in sound with another exchange name and, wherever possible, should have some relevance to the respective telephone area – no mean task in naming 255 exchanges!

An employee of the London Telephone Service, Miss J. M. McMillan, compiled a list of 23815 suggested names from which the final exchange names were selected – though often only after much bitter dispute between the local authority, tradespeople and residents and the Telephone Service; the inhabitants of Wapping, for example, were outraged that the numerical equivalent of their name was already assigned, but were placated by being given the exchange name, 'Royal'. The use of the new system was also not without its problems; there were stories of people dialling the first three letters and then shouting the rest of the number into the receiver in the expectation of being connected, while German immigrants attempting to call Wimbledon subscribers were often frustrated when dialling 'VIMbledon' did not achieve the desired result.

During their 30 years or so in service, the names of the London exchanges became so much a part of daily life that their passing (in the ten years from 1958, when all-figure numbers were introduced to enable the completion of the international STD system) was greatly lamented. The following list gives the names of all the old exchanges and the area exchange names and numbers that replaced them. The numerical prefix now used sometimes, but not always, corresponds to the numerical equivalent of the old dialable three-letter exchange name. If your current exchange number is not on the list, it must have come into existence after the change-over to all-figure numbers.

Original name	New exchange	Number
ABBey	Westminster	222
ACOrn	Acton	992
ADDiscombe	Addiscombe	654
ADVance	Mile End	980
ALBert Dock	Albert Dock	476
ALPerton	Perivale	998
AMBassador	Paddington	262
AMHerst	Hackney	985
ARChway	Upper Holloway	272
ARNold	North Wembley	904
ATLas	Isleworth	568
AVEnue	Monument	283
BALham	Balham	672
BARnet	Barnet	449
BATtersea	Battersea	228
BAYswater	Bayswater	229
BECkenham	Beckenham	650
BELgravia	Belgravia	235
BERmondsey	Bermondsey	237
BEXleyheath	Bexleyheath	303
BIShopsgate	Bishopsgate	247
BLUebell	Addiscombe	656
BOWes Park	Bowes Park	888
BRIxton	Brixton	274
BRUnswick	Kings Cross	278
BUCkhurst	Woodford	504
BUShey Heath	Bushey Heath	950
BYRon	South Harrow	422
BYWood	Purley	668
CANonbury	Canonbury	226
CENtral	Faraday	236
CHAncery	Holborn	242
CHErrywood	Merton Park	540
CHIswick	Chiswick	994
CITy	Faraday	248
CLErkenwell	Clerkenwell	253

Original name	New exchange	Number
CLIssold	Kingsland Green	254
CLOcktower	Upton Park	552
COLindale	Colindale	205
CONcord	South Harrow	864
COOmbe End	Malden	949
COPpermill	Walthamstow	520
COVent Garden	Covent Garden	240
CREscent	Gants Hill	550
CROydon	Croydon	688
CRYstal Palace	Sydenham	659
CUNningham	Lords	286
DANson Park	Bexleyheath	304
DERwent	Worcester Park	337
DICkens	Canonbury	359
DILigence	Wembley	903
DOLlis Hill	Cricklewood	450
DOMinion	Dagenham	592
DREadnought	Earls Court	371
DRUmmond	North Wembley	908
DRYden	Kingsbury	204
DUKe	Fulham	931
DUNcan	Rushey Green	690
EASt	Poplar	987
EALing	Ealing	567
EDGware	Edgware	952
EDMonton	Edmonton	807
ELGar	Harlesden	965
ELMbridge	Surbiton	399
EMBerbrook	Thames Ditton	398
ELStree	Elstree	953
ELTham	Eltham	850
EMPress	West Kensington	603
ENField	Enfield	363
ENTerprise	New Southgate	368
EUSton	Euston	387
EWEll	Ewell	393

Original name	New exchange	Number
FAIrlands	North Cheam	644
FELtham	Feltham	890
FIEld End	Pinner	868
FINchley	Finchley	346
FITzroy	Crouch End	348
FLAxman	Chelsea	352
FLEet Street	Fleet Street	353
FLOral	Mortlake	878
FOOts Cray	Sidcup	300
FORest Hill	Forest Hill	699
FOUntain	Streatham	677
FOX Lane	Palmers Green	882
FRAnklin	Wallington	669
FREmantle	Earls Court	373
FRObisher	Earls Court	370
FULham	Fulham	385
GALleon	Worcester Park	330
GEOrgian	Ealing	579
GERrard	Gerrard Street	437
GIBbon	Putney	789
GIPsy Hill	Gipsy Hill	670
GLAdstone	Cricklewood	452
GOOdmayes	Goodmayes	599
GRAngewood	Upton Park	472
GREenwich	Greenwich	858
GRImsdyke	Stanmore	954
GROsvenor	Mayfair	499
GULliver	Kentish Town	485
HADley Green	Barnet	440
HAInault	Hainault	500
HAMpstead	Hampstead	435
HARrow	Harrow	427
HATch End	Hatch End	428
HAYes	Hayes	573
HEAdquarters	Wood Street	432
HENdon	Hendon West	202

Original name	New exchange	Number
HIGhgate Wood	Muswell Hill	444
HILlside	North Finchley	445
HITher Green	Catford	698
HOGarth	Shepherds Bush	749
HOLborn	Holborn	405
HOP	Southwark	407
HOUnslow	Hounslow	570
HOWard	Ponders End	804
HUDson	Hounslow	572
HUNter	Marylebone	486
HURstway	Hayes Common	462
HYDe Park	Mayfair	493
ILFord	Ilford Central	478
IMPerial	Chislehurst	467
ISLeworth	Isleworth	560
IVAnhoe	Woodford	505
IVYdale	Ewell[1]	394
JUNiper	Primrose Hill	586
KEAts	Enfield	366
KELvin	South Clapham	673
KENsington	South Kensington	589
KILburn	Maida Vale	328
KINgston	Kingston	546
KIPling	Grove Park	857
KNIghtsbridge	South Kensington	584
LABurnum	Winchmore Hill	360
LADbroke	Kensal Green	969
LAKeside	Wimbledon	947
LANgham	Howland Street	580
LARkswood	Highams Park	527
LATimer	Stamford Hill	802
LEE Green	Lee Green	852
LEYtonstone	Leytonstone	539
LIBerty	Merton Park	542
LIVingstone	Beulah Hill	653

Original name	New exchange	Number
LONdon Wall	Wood Street	588
LORds	Lords	289
LOUghton	Loughton	508
LOWer Hook	Chessington	397
LTR	Vauxhall	587
LUDgate Circus	Faraday	583
MACaulay	Nine Elms	622
MAIda Vale	Maida Vale	624
MALden	Malden	942
MANsion House	Monument	626
MARyland	Stratford	534
MAYfair	Mayfair	629
MEAdway	Golders Green	458
MELville	Sutton Cheam	643
METropolitan	Moorgate	638
MILl Hill	Mill Hill	959
MINcing Lane	Monument	623
MITcham	Mitcham	648
MOLesey	Molesey	979
MONarch	Wood Street	606
MOOrgate	Wood Street	600
MOUntview	Crouch End	340
MULberry	Bowes Park	889
MUNicipal	Croydon	686
MUSeum	Howland Street	636
NATional	Moorgate	628
NEW Cross	New Cross	639
NOBle	West Kensington	602
NORth	Lower Holloway	607
NUFfield	Hayes	848
PADdington	Paddington	723
PALmers Green	Palmers Green	886
PARk	Bayswater	727
PECkham Rye	New Cross	732
PERivale	Perivale	997

Original name	New exchange	Number
PINner	Pinner	866
PLUmstead	Woolwich	855
POLlards	Norbury	764
POPesgrove	Twickenham	892
PRImrose	Primrose Hill	722
PROspect	Mortlake	876
PUTney	Putney	788
RAGlan	Leytonstone	556
RAVensbourne	Bromley	460
REDpost	Brixton	733
REGent	Gerrard Street	734
RELiance	Vauxhall	735
RENown	Parsons Green	736
RIChmond	Richmond Kew	940
RIPpleway	Barking	594
RIVerside	Hammersmith	748
RODney	Walworth	703
ROYal	Wapping	709
SANderstead	Sanderstead	657
SCOtt	Nine Elms	720
SEVen Kings	Goodmayes	590
SHEpherds Bush	Shepherds Bush	743
SHOreditch	Shoreditch	739
SILverthorne	Chingford	529
SKYport	Skyport	759
SLOane	Sloane	730
SNAresbrook	Wanstead	530
SOUthall	Southall	574
SPArtan	Kingsland Green	249
SPEedwell	Golders Green	455
SPRingpark	West Wickham	777
STAmford Hill	Stamford Hill	800
STEpney Green	Stepney Green	790
STOnegrove	North Edgware	958
STReatham	Streatham	769
SULlivan	Whitehall	799

Original name	New exchange	Number
SUNny Hill	Hendon East	203
SWIss Cottage	Hampstead	794
SYDenham	Sydenham	778
TATe Gallery	Pimlico	828
TEDdington Lock	Teddington	977
TEMple Bar	Covent Garden	836
TERminus	Kings Cross	837
THOrnton Heath	Thornton Heath	684
TIDeway	Deptford	692
TOTtenham	Tottenham	808
TOWnley	Dulwich	693
TRAfalgar	Whitehall	839
TREvelyan	Ilford Central	553
TROjan	Wandsworth	870
TUDor	Muswell Hill	883
TULse Hill	Tulse Hill	674
TURnham Green	Chiswick	995
TWIckenham Green	Kneller Hall	894
UNDerhill	Harrow	863
UPLands	Purley	660
UPPer Clapton	Clapton	806
VALentine	Ilford North	554
VANdyke	Wandsworth	874
VICtoria	Pimlico	834
VIGilant	Sutton Cheam	642
VIKing	Northolt	845
VIRginia	Finchley	349
WALlington	Wallington	647
WANstead	Wanstead	989
WARing Park	Sidcup	302
WATerloo	Southbank	928
WAXlow	Greenford	578
WELbeck	Marylebone	935
WEMbley	Wembley	902
WEStern	Kensington Gardens	937

Original name	New exchange	Number
WHItehall	Whitehall	930
WIDmore	Bromley	464
WILlesden	Willesden	459
WIMbledon	Wimbledon	946
WOOlwich	Woolwich	854
WORdsworth	Kenton Road	907

THE ORIGINS OF THE NAMES OF TEN LONDON TELEPHONE EXCHANGES

1 ACOrn

Acton, the area covered by the exchange, has the same numerical equivalent as Battersea, and thus could not be used. Acton Borough Council suggested 'Oaktown', the modern version of the Saxon word from which 'Acton' is derived, but as 'O' was dialled for the operator, no words beginning with it were acceptable. Acorn, as the fruit of the oak, was decided on as the next best name.

2 BYRon

This, the 1000th automatic telephone exchange in the country, was named after one of nearby Harrow School's most famous pupils – Lord Byron (1788–1824).

3 ENTerprise

The obvious local names of New Southgate and Southgate were rejected because of their numerical clash with New Cross and Southall. 'Enterprise' was chosen as an appropriate name for a rapidly growing neighbourhood.

4 FLAxman

The Chelsea exchange took its name from John Flaxman (1755–1826), the neoclassical sculptor. Although he had no direct connection with Chelsea, it was thought that his name was suitably 'artistic' and memorable.

5 GIBbon

Edward Gibbon was one of Putney's most notable inhabitants; the famous historian was born there in 1737.

6 KEAts

John Keats (1795–1821) was educated in Enfield from 1803–10.

7 LIVingstone

The missionary, David Livingstone (1813–73), was first encouraged to work in Africa by Robert Moffat, a resident of Norwood, whose daughter, Mary, Livingstone later married. This link was deemed sufficient – and his name suitably memorable – for the local exchange to be given his name.

8 MACaulay

Neither obvious local name – Stockwell and Larkhall – could be used as they were easily confused with Southall and Whitehall. The name 'Macaulay' was selected because the historian Lord Macaulay (1800–59) had an association with the area – his father, Zachary, was an eminent member of the 'Clapham Sect' and an opponent of slavery.

9 SPEedwell

M. C. Pink, the Deputy Director of the London Telephone Exchange, was given the task of finding a name for the Golders Green exchange after its own name was rejected as numerically identical to the first named automatic exchange, Holborn; fifty alternative names were also rejected by the local authority. Mulling over the name, Pink thought of the phrase 'gold as green'; he then considered what makes the colour gold or yellow turn green and came up with the answer, blue. What is one of the most vivid shades of blue? That of the flower, the speedwell. So, by this obscure train of thought, the name was suggested and accepted.

10 VIGilant

Sutton could not be used as it was numerically equivalent to Putney. Vigilant was chosen because it was the name of the stage coach which used to stop at Sutton on the daily London to Brighton route.

TWENTY LONDON ODDITIES

As the rest of this book shows, London is full of surprises. The final list is of twenty strange items that don't belong anywhere else:

1 London's oldest men?

The burial register of St Leonard's, Shoreditch, E1, records the death in 1588 of Thomas Cam – aged 207. Another aged Londoner, Thomas Parr, known as 'Old Parr', is commemorated by a memorial in Westminster Abbey. He allegedly died in 1635 aged 152.

2   Behind closed doors

Nos. 23–24 Leinster Gardens, W2, are not real houses; they form a façade to conceal the District and Circle Line railways behind.

3   St James's memorial

On the wall of St James's House, 23–24 King Street, SW1, is a relief depicting Laurence Olivier and Vivien Leigh, who managed the St James's Theatre on this site in the 1950s.

4   Porter's Rest

The peculiar plank of wood raised above the pavement on two metal supports on the Piccadilly side of Green Park is a 'Porter's Rest', erected in 1861 by the Vestry of St George, Hanover Square, at the suggestion of R. A. Slaney, MP, 'for the benefit of porters and others carrying burdens'.

5   Telemessage oddities

A number of London organizations have unusual cable (now 'Telemessage') addresses, such as: CATERWAUL (the feminist publishers, Virago Press Ltd, W1); HANDCUFFS (the Assistant Commissioner of Police, CID); PLATYPUS (Gerald Duckworth & Co Ltd, NW1) and TOUGHNESS (British Rawhide Belting Co Ltd, W1).

6   Heavenly view

In St Mary's New Church, Stoke Newington, N16, there is a somewhat incongruous stained glass depicting Jodrell Bank radio telescope.

7   Plague prediction

In a pamphlet published in 1648, the astrologer William Lilly predicted that around 1665 there would be a fate 'ominous to London . . . by reason of sundry fires and a consuming plague'. The Great Plague hit London in 1665; in 1666 the Great Fire broke out.

8   Coronation graffiti

The Coronation Chair, made for Edward I and one of the most venerated treasures of Westminster Abbey, is defaced by graffiti: it has carved on its back, 'Peter Abbott slept in this chair, July 5, 1800'. Abbott is presumed to have been a Westminster schoolboy who occupied his hands with a penknife during a long service.

9   Pier cross

The crucifix on the wall of St Etheldreda, Fulham, SW6, was made by Rita Lang with wood from Brighton Pier.

10   Sedan phone

If you use the telephone in Shepherd's Tavern, 50 Hertford Street, W1, you will find yourself inside the eighteenth-century sedan chair that once belonged to the Duke of Cumberland.

11   Mother Goose laid to rest

In the registers of the church of St Olave, Hart Street, EC3, there is a record of the burial on 14 September 1586 of Mother Goose.

12   Innocent mice

One of the buildings in Philpot Lane, EC3, has a carving of two mice on it. There are several explanations for this, one of which is that it commemorates the death of a craftsman working on the building. He had been accused by another of eating his sandwiches and pushed off the roof – his accuser then found that the 'thief' was a mouse.

13   Heroes' glory

Postmen's Park, EC1, contains a collection of monuments to heroes and heroines – some of them children – who lost their lives saving others.

14 An ex-parrot
The oldest stuffed bird in England is probably the parrot exhibited in Westminster Abbey with the effigy of Frances Stuart, Duchess of Richmond and Lennox. The parrot died shortly after the Duchess, in 1702, having lived with her for over 40 years. Frances Stuart was the model for Britannia on coinage at the time of Charles II, and allegedly one of his few unrequited loves.

15 Recycling
A street lamp just off the Strand was once lit with gas from the sewer beneath.

16 Dr Barry's secret
Buried in Kensal Green Cemetery, NW10, are the remains of Dr James Barry, an eminent army doctor and Inspector General of Hospitals, who died in 1865. After his death, it was discovered that 'James' was actually a woman. By posing as a man all her adult life, she became the first qualified woman doctor in Britain.

17 Camouflage
The telephone kiosk on the Embankment near Waterloo Bridge is uniquely painted green, because it is on land owned by the Institute of Electrical Engineers who in 1928 granted it to the GPO on condition that the kiosk was painted to match surrounding railings and to blend in with the nearby garden.

18 Animals at peace
There is a pet's cemetery at Victoria Gate, Hyde Park. The epitaphs include ones to 'My Wee Pet Monte', 'My Sweet Baby Quita' and 'In Loving Memory of Puskin and Fluff-Fluff'.

19 Whitebait dinners
Whitebait were once caught in shoals at Blackwall and Greenwich, and Whitebait Dinners were held annually from the early eighteenth century until 1894, often attended by notable political figures.

216

20 Determinedly final
The last name in the London Telephone Directory is B. I.
Zzytt, who recently ousted Z. Z. Zzitz – a pseudonym created
for this purpose.

BIBLIOGRAPHY

The seemingly large number of books I have consulted is just a tiny fraction of the colossal total literature of London. To begin to do it justice would take another book as long as this. To those who want to delve further, I recommend the libraries of the Guildhall and the GLC, the London Library (members only, but well worth the subscription) and the local history collections of London's public libraries. It would be appropriate, however, to offer my personal list of:

THE TEN BEST BOOKS ON LONDON

1 Felix Barker and Ralph Hyde, *London as it Might Have Been* (John Murray, 1982)
   An entertaining view of London's 'buildings that were never built'.

2 Felix Barker and Peter Jackson, *London: 2000 Years of a City and its People* (Macmillan, 1974; 1984)
   The best general illustrated history of London.

3 David Benedictus, *The Essential Guide to London* (Sphere Books, 1984)
   A personal selection of some often quirky London bests and worsts.

4 Caroline Dakers, *The Blue Plaque Guide to London* (Macmillan, 1981)
   A thorough guide to the houses of London's most famous and infamous inhabitants.

5 Ian Hessenberg (ed.), *The London Book* (Bergstrom and Boyle, 1980)
   A now sadly out of print picture book of London's architectural features and oddities.

6 Hermione Hobhouse, *Lost London* (Macmillan, 1979)
   The key book on the major buildings in London that have been swept away in the name of progress.

7 Sir Nikolaus Pevsner, *London 1: The Cities of London and Westminster; London 2: South* (Penguin, 1957; 1952)

The standard reference work on the architecture of London.

8 Edward Jones and Christopher Woodward, *A Guide to the Architecture of London* (Weidenfeld & Nicolson, 1983)
An award-winning handbook, essential for any would-be London explorer.

9 William Kent, *An Encyclopedia of London* (J. M. Dent, 1951)
An oddly organized but generally useful reference book.

10 Ben Weinreb and Christopher Hibbert, *The London Encyclopaedia* (Macmillan, 1983)
Without qualification, the best book on London ever published.